101

uses for a

PENCIL

101
uses for a
PENCIL

Peter Gray

NEW
HOLLAND

Dedicated to my lovely wife, Clare
(who has another use for a pencil I couldn't possibly reveal here).

Introduction

There's nothing special about the pencil is there? As far as tools go, it's just about as lowly as you can get. Pencils are just there. You've got a drawer full of them and you don't even know where they all came from—and yet there's never one to hand when you need one. And they get blunt, and the shavings get all over the tablecloth, and it really hurts when you tread on one in bare feet. No, nothing much to get excited about…

But consider for a moment the marvel of this simple tool. This is the first tool you ever learned to handle. It has been the tool of choice for artists throughout the ages. Many of the great novels and poems were first set down in pencil. World-changing inventions and designs took shape at the point of the pencil. The pencil is resistant to moisture, chemicals, light degradation and aging, and yet its mark can be easily erased with a piece of rubber. It requires no batteries, no user's guide, and no online support. The pencil has only one moving part: it. Yes it is simple, but that is its genius. In capable hands it can achieve wonders.

This book will show you how artists use the pencil to perform feats that sometimes seem like alchemy, turning blank paper into 'art'. Or perhaps you yourself would like to be able to draw. Most people do; it's nothing to be ashamed of. This book will prove that it is within your reach to do genuinely impressive things with nothing more than a pencil and the courage to wield it.

There is no drawing tool so responsive, subtle, versatile… or cheap. But the pencil's versatility also extends well into the less expressive areas of our lives, with all manner of practical, entertaining and frivolous uses. This book aims to explore how the humble pencil may help us to fulfil our creative urges, to communicate with our fellow human, to ease some of life's little glitches and to bring us some good old-fashioned fun. By dipping into this book you will soon agree that, even in the modern age, the pencil surely retains its point.

2B or not 2B?

I suppose we had better have a little think about what pencils are and what sorts you can get. A pencil is just a wooden stick with some lead running through it, right? Actually, they are made of a finely ground mineral called graphite compounded with clay, which is baked and encased in a particular type of wood called incense cedar. This marvellous soft wood, native to western states of North America, is chosen for its aromatic qualities, its degree of softness for easy sharpening and its resistance to splintering.

Pencils as we know them today can be traced back to 1564, when a huge graphite deposit was discovered in Borrowdale, in Cumbria, England. This substance was initially mistaken for lead ore, hence the misnomer, but it is in fact a form of carbon (the same stuff that we puny humans are made of). For many centuries the Cumbria mine remained the sole source of pure graphite. It remains very much in use to this day and at nearby Keswick, where there is a museum devoted entirely to pencils (www.pencilmuseum.co.uk).

Powdered graphite is mixed with clay in varying ratios resulting in different grades of pencil. Graphite is soft and makes a black mark so 'B' stands for 'Black'. Clay is hard and makes no mark of its own so 'H' stands for 'Hard'. Where the two are in equal measure the pencil is graded HB—this is your standard workhorse pencil, issued by the million to school children and office workers. This grade is sometimes known as 'F', but no one remembers what the F stands for.

Beyond HB is a spectrum of grades ranging from 9H (very hard, almost invisible), to 9B (smudges if you only look at it). The number denotes the degree of hardness or blackness.

Hard pencils make faint marks and keep their points for a long time. One hard pencil (H or 2H is quite hard enough) will last you most of your lifetime. The legendary cartoonist Albert Underzo used only a single hard pencil when drawing draw Asterix and Cleopatra but got through 62 soft pencils. Soft pencils are much more satisfying. 2B is a good standard drawing pencil (used for most of the drawings in this book) and you may like to augment it with, say, a 4B and a 6B.

For many activities, it could be said that a pencil is only as good as its point. For general

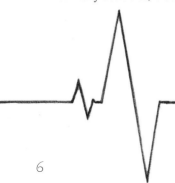

use, a little manual pencil sharper is a worthy tool, as long it's sharp. It is infinitely more satis-fying to whittle a point with a sharp knife, which can also facilitate sharpening a longer length of lead, useful for drawing with. There are purists who work through grades of sandpaper to achieve surgically precise points, but this looks rather like prevarication to me.

TIP: Try to avoid dropping or otherwise mistreating your pencils. You can easily break the lead inside, which becomes apparent when the lead falls out in chunks while sharpening.

And we must say a few words about rubbers, or 'erasers' as we're supposed to call them nowadays. In the eighteenth century, one of the first uses anyone found for this new material was rubbing out pencil marks. So rubber was named after the action; it is no mere etymolog-ical accident. Do not feel shy of rubbing out mistakes. It's an essential part of the drawing process, so get yourself a good rubber. There are hard 'plastic' erasers, soft India rubber erasers, pliable 'putty' erasers and even electric erasers. I reckon pretty much any eraser will do. If you buy one from an art shop, it should be of adequate quality.

TIP: Erasers that become rounded down can be reshaped with a knife or cut in two at a jaunty angle to make two halves with pointed corners.

For most of the entries in this book you'll need nothing more than your trusty pencil. Okay, you may need a rubber, but that's it. Oh, and some paper. Don't get het up about paper; any old cheap stuff will do for most purposes. You are about to embark on a journey with your pencil. On that journey you will get into some scrapes and that's good—it means you're pushing yourself. If you are worried about spoiling reams of expensive art paper, you won't feel the freedom to let your pencil lead you down untrodden paths.

Right, that's quite enough pencillious preamble—down to business.

001   Annotate a Book

When textbooks were handed out at school, our eager young minds somehow managed to resist the enticing facts for at least for as long as it took to check out the rude drawings and libellous comments left by previous recipients. We haven't grown up much since then. Presented with notes scrawled in a book, we are still impotent to ignore them. Notes are records of thought processes and thoughts are interesting.

Annotating a book allows you to refer back to the bits that inspired you and to remind you of the ideas that they sparked. What, after all, is a book for? To inform, to illuminate, to entertain—not to be preserved in mint condition until you eventually kick the bucket and your soulless son-in-law dumps it in a bin bag.

So why not start with this book? If you find your thoughts running to ideas, jot them down. If you feel moved to underscore parts of the text, I'll be very flattered. Draw on top of the guidelines and grids of the demonstrations. Doodle in the margins. Add your own embellishments to my drawings. Turn the book into an artefact. Make it yours.

002   Make Some Marks

'Mark making' is a term used by artists to mean the marks made by a pencil on paper. It may sound too obvious to mention, but those marks can vary greatly in quality and feel and produce a multitude of effects for texture, shading, atmosphere, decoration and so on.

Making marks on paper is a pleasure that is deeply rooted in us all: A tiny child takes a stick and bangs it. It makes a sound and she is pleased. Exchange the stick for a pencil and . . . what's this? A mark! Soon dots become lines, lines become shapes and before long images appear, as she settles into her new role of creator.

It's a shame that some of us have forgotten this childish thrill. There is nothing wrong with being childlike—Picasso spent most of his career trying to recapture the joyous abandon that comes naturally to children. The funny thing is that making bold pencil marks is not only deeply satisfying but it is also a sure route to confident and competent draughtsmanship. Too often, amateurs approach a drawing with anxiety, and use hesitant, whispery marks that will only ever result in hesitant, whispery drawings.

How long is it since you scribbled and scrawled just for fun? When no one is looking, take a wodge of scrap paper and attack it with your pencil in every way you can think of: thick lines, thin lines, wavy lines, jagged lines, shapes, dots, slabs. Make them heavy or delicate, use the pencil's tip, change your grip, use the side, smudge, scribble and shade. Make a mess and enjoy the sensation of pushing the soft black graphite across virgin white paper.

You probably felt little hesitation as you made your marks. If you set out to draw a straight line, you set it down quickly and confidently and it turned out pretty well, for a straight line. You are already becoming master of your pencil; remember this and aim to make a similar statement of confidence with every mark that you draw.

(003) The Levitating Pencil Trick

When you know how this trick is done it seems incredible that anyone can actually fall for it. But performed with spontaneous elegance, it can often catch people off guard, and it will leave small kids scratching their heads for ages.

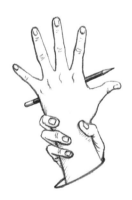

Show the audience an ordinary pencil (a long one) and your empty left palm. Lay the pencil across your palm, grip it with a firm fist and then turn your hand over so that the back faces upwards. Now make a bit of a show of pulling back your left sleeve (to show that you have nothing hidden there) and clasp under your left wrist with your right hand. What the audience sees next is that you fully open your clenched left fist, but the pencil does not drop to the floor, it remains stuck to the underside of your hand. What the audience does not know is that you had previously slipped your right index finger into your left fist to hold the pencil in place.

As long as you keep your left hand angled downwards, screening any view of the offending finger, and then move swiftly onto your next trick, you stand a good chance of the penny failing to drop with your awestruck audience.

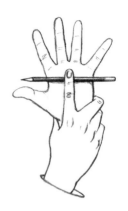

 # 004 Multiple Line Sketching

Aspiring draughtspersons are often put off when drawings fail to fall easily and cleanly into place. But it must be noted that even the most experienced artists find the ideal lines and marks frustratingly elusive at times. So don't beat yourself up. In fact, you could turn your hesitant marks into a virtue by adopting the appropriate technique.

A common drawing method used by no less a draughtsman than Leonardo Da Vinci is to draw loosely around the contours of a subject using multiple lines. The idea is that no one line provides a definitive edge, but rather the drawing emerges out of a profusion of approximate marks. As well as freeing you to draw without inhibition, this approach produces lively drawings that can also be suggestive of motion. I drew this picture from a terracotta statue of an Indian goddess—a very solid and static object. But the vigorously scrawling marks make the figure seem to shimmy and dance and possess weightlessness beyond the source material.

A drawing does not have to be brought into life with a struggle. If there is joy in its creation, that will usually translate into the finished piece.

Imagine you are out and about and you spot a dainty little cabinet that would look just peachy in your empty alcove, or a tasteful antique frame that would suit one of your masterful drawings. Before handing over your precious cash, you'll probably want to measure such an item to make sure it will fit. So, assuming you don't habitually carry a tape measure in your handbag or man-bag, what will you do?

Whip out your pencil and make the necessary measurements in pencil lengths. It doesn't matter how long your pencil is because when you get home you can simply measure the pencil and multiply its length by the number of pencil lengths used in your original measurements. Now, if only you had something with which to jot down the measurements...

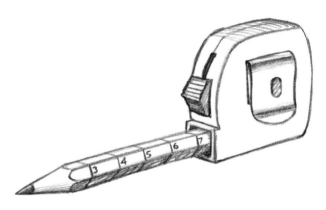

(006) Draw Imprecise Subjects

Getting a basic drawing 'right' can be a big hang-up for beginners to drawing. But much effort and heartache can be spared with a cunning choice of subject matter. We may judge a portrait by its likeness, a figure by its proportions and articulation, a building by its perspective, but who is to judge how large a parsnip should be relative to an onion, or whether you have accurately captured the contours of a particular rock or tree?

Working with subjects of indefinite size and shape (or 'form') allows for free and easy drawing practice, without the worry that it may end up looking 'wrong'. Let's have a look at this in practice:

For this quick demo, I organised the random (and slightly manky) vegetables that were languishing in my kitchen into a pleasing arrangement and then jotted down their rough masses and shapes. If you try this yourself, make the drawing a good size on the paper (mine is about 25 centimetres across) and do it quickly. With virtually no effort you will already have the bones of a drawing.

Once the basic shapes are set down you can look a bit more carefully and hone the rough shapes here and there as necessary. Again it should not take long because there is no need for precision.

From there it's a quick and easy process to erase the scruffy marks and mistakes and refine the outlines of your vegetables. Do not worry about describing every knobble and ridge, just try to capture something of the particular characters of the outlines. Give yourself no more than fifteen minutes and if it doesn't come out so great, start again rather than slaving away at the same drawing.

Now, before you carry your veg away to the stew pot, you may like to refer to them to add texture (012) and shading (018).

Col

This is a super-simple game for two, devised by a man called Colin, based around the idea of claiming territories on a 'map'. The map need be nothing more than a hastily scribbled doodle of crisscrossing lines and shapes. Any old shapes will do, although there is no harm in aiming for a degree of aesthetic merit. You are perfectly at liberty to trace all the states of the USA, but the game would not work any better for it.

The players take turns to shade parts of the map in their own distinctive shading pattern (hatching in different directions works well, but as long as the two players' marks can be easily distinguished, feel free to express yourselves). The restriction is that no player may claim two adjoining regions. They are allowed to touch at a point but not along a border. The first player to be unable to claim a new territory is the LOOOOSER!!!

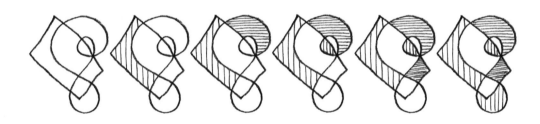

Guidelines and Construction Lines

We may imagine the artist squinting at his subject though a wine-soaked haze and casually recording every contour and detail with superhuman precision. But in reality, artists need to put in a bit of prep work, just as any craftsman does. It doesn't take much—a few simple guidelines can quickly establish a kind of rough scaffold, upon which the finer shapes and details may be hung with relative ease. And because pencil is so easy to erase, it's the perfect medium for any amount of construction lines that may be deemed useful.

Let us look at drawing of a simple jug. For clarity of demonstration I have drawn quite heavily here, but generally guidelines should be quite faint, perhaps drawn with a harder pencil, such as H. This subject is not without its complexity, but in its basic form it is essentially a cylinder. I started with a vertical centre line, which helps to map out the object symmetrically. Then I sketched the ellipses for the top and bottom of the jug. It's not easy to draw an ellipse, but going over the lines repeatedly soon produces a good approximation of the shape (see 004). Although only the front edge of the bottom ellipse will survive in the finished drawing, it makes for a more convincing shape if you draw the ellipse in full to start with. I then joined up the ellipses to form the sides of the jug and lastly marked a diagonal line across the top, so that I could place the handle and spout directly opposite each other.

Over my rough construction lines I can then draw the upper and lower rims of the jug and add the spout and handle.

Once happy with the overall form, I can carefully erase all the guidelines and scrappy marks. Then, using a softer pencil or working with bolder marks, the drawing can be finally set down with smooth, confident outlines.

Draw a Line in the Sand

In a literal sense, a pencil is as good a tool as any for drawing a line in the sand. Figuratively speaking, though, the phrase means 'to define a limit or boundary; to state a level of tolerance beyond which one will not go'. Anyone sharing a flat will understand the necessity of such limits being defined. With a pencil you can label your cheese, annotate a phone bill, jot cheery reminders about washing the dishes, putting out the bins, buying the milk and so on.

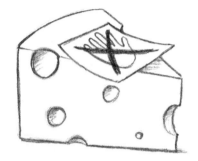

Such messages need to be communicated, but they can look somewhat confrontational if stated verbally. There's something about words that can rub people up the wrong way, even in written form. Symbols and drawings seem somehow friendlier means of communication, as if you've taken the trouble to cheer someone up with a nice picture, rather than condemn their idleness. A spoonful of sugar helps the medicine go down. Your pencil is a tool of domestic harmony.

 # Portraits in Profile

Drawing portraits is always a favourite subject, especially if you surround yourself with beautiful people. It's not without its difficulties, but you can ease yourself into this rewarding discipline by placing a convenient limitation on your ambition. By far the easiest way to approach portraiture is to start with side views or 'profiles'.

First, some basic proportions: The adult head fits quite neatly into a square, the upper half of which is occupied almost entirely by the semi-circular dome of the skull. The eye sits half way down the head and the ear sits half way back, roughly level at the top with the eyebrow and at the bottom with the base of the nose. The nose protrudes outside of the square, as does the chin, which curves into the jaw-line, ending at the base of the ear. Note that the eye is a mere triangle from a profile view.

Now you know what a profile should roughly look like, you can turn your pencil to drawing real people how they really look. It can be helpful at first to start with a rough template head and draw your subject onto it. This handsome boy (he takes after his father) is not too far off the template. His eyes are quite deep-set, his nose a little shorter and his lower face slopes back a little, but essentially it's just about drawing the shapes of his features and hair onto the standard head.

This roguish old dude is a different matter. At a more advanced age, the square jaw of youth is no longer quite so taught. So the neckline hangs low and it's decorated with some jowly details. Men's ears never stop growing (did you know that?) and Dad's are shaping up quite impressively. As well as his receded hairline, there are also wrinkles and character lines that make up the look he's going for, these days.

The very same template works just as well for ladies' heads, although their features are bound to be more delicate and refined. The main differences are slight: typically ladies will have a more prominent forehead with a less defined indentation at the bridge of the nose, an inward slope to the lower face and a more gently rounded jaw-line.

If you pay close attention to the individual features of your subjects and, crucially, the spaces in between them, you should, with a little practice, be able to transform a bland profile template into recognisable likenesses. And if a likeness goes astray, you've got your friendly eraser to bring things back on track.

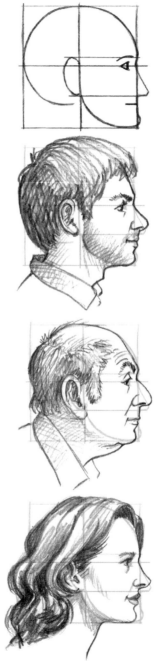

The Thumbaround Pencil Spin

There's something impressive about a pencil spinning deftly around in the hand. Even though we may have opinions about the cocky show-offs who casually perform these feats, deep down we secretly covet their skills (see also 061). The Thumb-around is probably the easiest such trick to master, though no less impressive for it. Essentially, the pencil is flicked with the fingers to circumnavigate the thumb and arrive safely back in your grasp

A fairly long pencil is required for this trick. Hold it tightly near the blunt end, between the thumb, index and ring fingers. Flick your ring finger inwards, as if clicking your fingers. This action will give your pencil the necessary momentum.

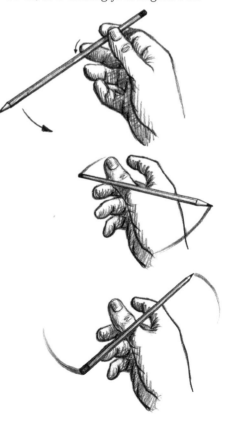

Throughout the whole action it is important that your thumb remains motionless. It is the fingers that do the work. If you have managed to propel the pencil with the correct degree of force, it will rotate quite merrily in a full circle around your thumb. That's the easy bit.

As a result of the initial flicking action, your index finger should naturally extend. If not, get into the habit of straightening it immediately after the flick. After a nanosecond or two the pencil will complete its transit, at which point you must curl your index finger back in to make the catch.

All things being well, the pencil will come to rest in a comfortable writing grip and you can get down to some immediate doodling without further adjustments, confident in the knowledge that your dexterity will not have gone unnoticed— you cocky show-off.

At first you will feel all fingers and thumbs.

The main thing is to flick the pencil round at the correct speed—too slow and it will falter, too fast and you will send it spinning into space. After a while you should be able to perform this feat without a moment's thought. You may even find yourself doing it unconsciously in idle moments or while you ponder a knotty problem.

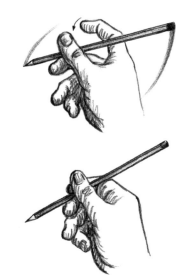

TIP: Sit on the floor to practice finger-spinning tricks. There is less chance of flying pencils getting lost and you won't have so far to go to pick them up. A quantity of practice pencils will also minimise your retrieval efforts.

 # 012 Drawing Texture

There are many ways to raise a drawing beyond the simplistic or mediocre, to give it the sheen of accomplishment and a feeling of realness. We have looked at drawing things in terms of their basic forms and proportions, all of which are completely valid, but there is much more to be delved into. Wherever you happen to be right now, look around at all the different textures that make up your environment. Unless you're reading this from a padded cell, every direction you look in will reveal distinct and seductive surfaces aching to be stroked and fondled by the naked eye. Perhaps you have never paid very much attention to textures, but the more you look, the more you will see that the world is rich with them, infinite in variety.

The pencil is a remarkable tool, capable of great subtleties of mark making. But here's the thing: you don't need to use it with great subtlety to convey an enormous range of textural sensations. A lot can be said with a few marks, just so long as they are of the appropriate quality. Let's return to the vegetables we drew in 006. There we arrived at an outline drawing with all the elements reasonably well shaped and proportioned. Just as we saw when drawing their shapes, precision is not important here—what matters is ascribing to each vegetable the right kind of texture.

In this stage I have actually added very little, but the marks on each vegetable are sufficiently distinctive to give the viewer a whole lot more information about them and how they differ from each other. The onion has filaments running straight up its sides from root to shoot. Being broadly spherical, however, the lines must be drawn to show its curvature, wrapping around the form. Its cousins, the leeks have soft, fluted lines running along their tubular lengths. Conversely, the ridges on the parsnip curve around its length and they are deeper and less even. You could drive yourself mad drawing all the speckled flowers on a head of broccoli. So don't. All that is required is a few textural marks

sprinkled around to hint at its distinctive surface. The viewer will be quite happy to fill in the blanks in his mind's eye.

If you embrace texture it will soon become an instinctive part of your drawing style and you will find yourself using texturally descriptive marks in everything you draw. Here is a dusty old dude I sketched from a dusty old portrait bust in a dusty old museum. Though the original is made of ceramic, gentle textural marks translate the curves and forms into a drawing of soft and yielding hair and flesh.

013 Join the Dots Puzzle

This is a deceptively tricky puzzle to challenge any chums who need taking down a peg or two. Present them with nine dots forming a three by three square. All they have to do is connect all the dots using no more than four straight lines . . . without lifting the pencil off the paper. It's as simple as that.

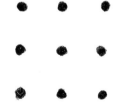

Try it yourself . . . not so easy is it? When everyone has had a few failed attempts and they are feeling somewhat less pleased with themselves you can reveal the solution. It requires a smidgen of lateral thinking:

Start in a top corner and draw a diagonal to the opposite corner. Your second line will get your mates kicking themselves. It goes straight up and continues *beyond the top of the box*. A third line then runs diagonally down through the top centre dot and the middle side dot, extending again outside the box. A direct horizontal completes the solution.

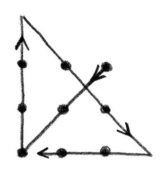

(014) Draw the Human Head

We spend so much time looking at faces that you would think we know what they look like. The truth is that we are preconditioned to merely judge reactions and read expressions. Children's drawings give us some clues as to how we perceive faces. I gave my children the brief to draw a realistic man's face. They both placed the eyes near the top of the head and made the mouths overlarge. These are the parts of the face that most clearly communicate emotion. Noses are minimal, ears an afterthought and no concern at all is given to chins, jaw-lines, cheekbones, foreheads or character lines.

Surely we notice more than children—but do we? Our familiarity with faces makes it hard for us to see them afresh for accurate drawing. Some basic proportions and guidelines can help. Seen from the front, a head can be thought of as basically oval and the features symmetrically arranged, so a template head should start with an egg shape with a neat vertical guideline drawn down the centre. A horizontal line sits half way down the head and another bisects the lower half again.

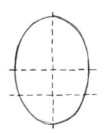

The eyes sit on the halfway line, much lower than many people assume. In terms of width, they each occupy about a fifth of the overall head width, with an eye's width either side and in between. Eyebrows go in just above the eyes and provide a level for the tops of the ears. The bottoms of the ears are level with the bottom of the nose. A neat triangle serves as a good guide for the width of the nose and mouth.

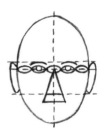

Now it gets a little trickier. With the head turned slightly to the side, for a three-quarter view, the vertical guideline has to curve over the brow and project down for the placement of nose and mouth. The features shift round too—the chin becomes more prominent and the ear swings into clear view. Things are further complicated when the head is tilted up or down, making it necessary too for horizontal guidelines too to curve around the form of the head.

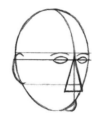

So there we have some simple templates, well enough proportioned to put them to immediate use. The proportions are the same for male or female adults, but the differences between the sexes are quite strong when you look carefully at the individual features. These two 'ideal' faces were both drawn over the same template. Wider eyes, smaller nose, finer eyebrows and so on make the lady clearly more feminine, but the greatest differences are in the outlines of the faces and jaw-lines and the broadness of the necks.

Templates such as these teach us the general proportions of the head, but of course, real faces differ greatly. Individuals may have short noses, prominent chins, flabby jowls, lop-sided smiles and all manner of idiosyncrasies and deformities than need to be observed and accounted for in your drawing. However hideous they may be, you'll find that your relatives are rather attached to their faces. Even though they may not be aware of their head's proportions in theory, they can tell at a glance when you've drawn them incorrectly. And won't they let you know it. But you must harden yourself to such judgement and not be discouraged; with practice you'll find likenesses will come more naturally

TIP: The less fussy and detailed you make your portrait drawings, the more elegant they will look and the more your subjects will feel flattered by the outcomes. Only draw the wrinkles that are very prominent and ignore the others.

(015) Pricking Out Seedlings

Prick out in the garden shed. This statement, of course, refers to the essential horticultural task of separating and re-potting seedlings after they have germinated in a seed tray. The tiny plants will need their own space to establish a strong root system and should ideally be pricked out as soon as the first 'true leaves' emerge (i.e., the second set of leaves after germination). For this task, the humble pencil is the ideal shape and size and used by professional gardeners.

Clear a good space on the workbench and prepare your pots or cellular seed trays with potting compost firmed in well and watered so that it's just moist. Insert your pencil into the compost and wiggle it around to make holes large enough to accommodate the new plants.

Select the strongest seedlings to transplant. One plant at a time, grasp gently by the leaves (never hold by the stem or roots) and use your pencil to ease the plant out of the seed tray, retaining as much root and soil as possible.

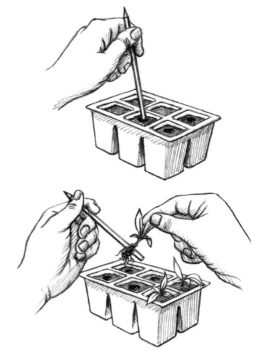

Resting the roots on your pencil, transfer the seedling to its new container. Lightly firm in the soil around the plant with your pencil, making sure that the leaves are just above the compost level. Don't worry if they go in a bit wonky—as long as they are the right way up, Mother Nature will soon have them growing straight and strong.

When all seedlings are transplanted, water them in with a fine watering rose and place them on a windowsill to receive sunlight and warmth. Finally, you'll need to label the plants. Use plastic plant labels or old ice-lolly sticks, pushed into the compost. If you write in pencil, it can later be erased later for re-use with another plant.

016 Tracing

When I was a schoolboy, just a few years ago (ahem), we frequently felt the need to transfer drawings onto different pieces of paper or pages of our exercise books. We employed all sorts of long-winded tracing methods, wearing our pencils down to stubs and covering everything in smudgy fingerprints. The scruffy results of these efforts satisfied our simple needs, but they were really quite artless.

Now that we have photocopiers and computer printers you would think that tracing has had its day. And surely it is beneath the dignity of an artist to trace. Ah, but think again. An artist will employ whatever method it takes to produce the desired results. It is common practice for artists and illustrators to draw rough versions of artworks before embarking on a finished piece. Why laboriously redraft an image when you have done it once already? A re-drafted image rarely re-captures the charm of the original. And so we trace.

Most professionals use a light box, a large flat box with an electric light inside and a translucent upper surface. Onto this the rough drawing is fixed and a fresh sheet of paper lain on top. The light

24

shines through both sheets, revealing the drawing and allowing for easy and accurate tracing. The upper sheet can also be moved around to reposition parts of the rough composition as required.

Outside of the professional studio tracing may also prove useful. You may do a sketch that you're quite pleased with but it has come out rather scruffy, or it has a nasty mistake or some distracting details. There is only so much you can clean up an eraser.

Of course you haven't got a light box. Or have you? Actually, there's one in every room of your home. Use some masking tape to fix your sketch and clean paper to a window, and the daylight streaming through will illuminate just as well as any light box. Tempting though it may be to trace the outlines with a hard pencil and polish it off at the desk, it makes for cleaner results to draw the finished line directly, at the tracing stage. Once all the necessary details are confidently traced, you can return to the desktop and develop the drawing as you see fit.

(017) Decorate Your Ears

For pencil enthusiasts there's a very good reason why we should delay the wearing of spectacles for as long as possible, for reasons that will become apparent.

We have seen, and will continue to see, how very useful it is to have a pencil permanently at the ready. Jacket pockets are okay, but you will often have to fish around ungracefully when the pencil falls horizontal or slips into the lining. Trouser pockets are prone to cause snappings and/or stabbings when you bend over. And keeping a pencil in a bag will simply not do, unless you enjoy emptying the entire contents in search of small objects. Ears are much more convenient and perfectly suited to the task.

Slipping a pencil behind the ear will keep it ready for immediate use and make you stand out as the studious and practical person you are. The sad thing is that this simple technique is not possible for anyone who wears glasses. Poor old Vincent van Gogh would have had a bit of trouble with it too. (Technically, I suppose, this tip should really be published under 101 Uses For an Ear.)

Light and Shading

Without light there can be no drawing. It is the stuff that makes subjects visible, that gives them form and depth and imbues them with atmosphere. The pencil cannot draw light, but it can suggest its presence by drawing the areas of shade that light cannot reach.

Let's look at this in stages: Returning to our casserole ingredients from 006 and 012, we have a set of forms that look reasonably well proportioned and textured, though distinctly lacking in substance. Because I drew them in the garden on a sunny day the light was strong, making the shadows very dark and crisp—perfect. So, to begin adding any shade I had to draw the shapes of the shadows cast by the objects. With the light coming slightly from behind, the shadows were cast into the foreground and make a pleasing set of shapes. Shadows also fall on some of the vegetables, curving around their rounded forms.

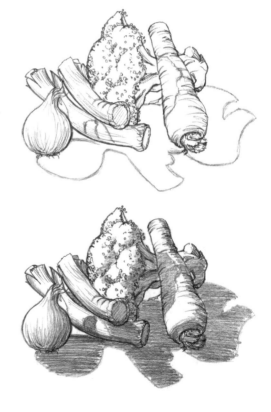

With such a strong set of shadows to work with the shading can start off quite crudely. With the side of a soft pencil I roughly filled in all the areas of shadow with a uniform layer of tone.

As is often the case with drawing, we reserve the best bit for last. I looked more closely at the areas of shade to identify the very darkest parts. Here I deepened the shading with my very darkest marks, in order to capture the greatest possible tonal range in the drawing. Then it was all about refining the varying degrees of shade, working across the picture as a whole.

TIP: It is quite easy to discern the degrees of shade if you look at the subject with squinted eyes.

I also observed those areas where light bounced back off surrounding objects to partially illuminate the undersides of vegetables, such as the onion, and used an eraser to lift off some of the pencil marks. Capturing this 'reflected light' can be very effective in drawings of light and shade.

TIP: Where light is the subject of a drawing it is a good idea to ignore 'local tone' (inherent tonal values, such as the darker green of the broccoli here) and concentrate entirely on the light and shade.

019 Scratch Your Back

'What a piece of work is a man! How noble in reason, how infinite in faculty! In form and moving how express and admirable! In action how like an Angel!' The human body is really rather well designed, but it is also prone… The human body is beautifully constructed to perform functions of remarkable power and delicacy. But it is also prone to bothersome niggles, one of which is the itch, right in the middle of your back, that your infinitely capable limbs just cannot reach. In the absence of a willing accomplice, the pencil can be used to extend your reach just far enough to settle the matter and find the bliss you crave. And using the pointy end it can even penetrate a thick pullover, though you may suffer some scribble marks on the back of your crisp, white shirt.

Caricature by Tracing

Achieving a recognisable likeness can be difficult. Oh, the hours I have spent, the pencils I have worn to a nub, searching for that indefinable spark of individual character in a face. So you would think that perpetrating gross distortions on a personality would make the task yet harder . . . but you might be surprised; exaggerating prominent features can make it a whole lot easier to set down a likeness. And the challenge can be further lessened by following the following lesson.

Hone your skill on personalities who have a very strong image. That way, even if the likeness goes astray you will still have certain landmark features (Einstein's mad hair and moustache, Churchill's hat and cigar) to inform the viewer. Start off with profiles—we've seen how easy they are to draw (see 010). And to really get things moving, trace (see 016). Tracing may seem like cheating, but your drawing skills are not at test here so much as your interpretations.

Here's a tracing I did of Elvis. Everyone loves Elvis. I printed off a photo at a good size and placed some layout paper over the top. Layout paper is what animators use to trace characters repeatedly. It's very thin, so you can see a picture through it—it's also very useful and very cheap.

With another sheet of layout paper on top I could see through to my original drawing and trace it through. The difference at this stage is that I moved the paper around and tweaked some features here and there as I traced the face. I started by tracing the eyebrow and then moved the paper to the left, just a touch, to set the eye deeper. In tracing the nose I raised the paper slightly, to make the nose smaller. Although I exaggerated the lips, working on top of the earlier drawing made it easy to copy their shapes through at a larger scale.

Now for the rest of the head. All the juicy bits are at the front of the head; no one's interested in the back, so it can be diminished greatly, and easily by moving the layout paper over to the right. I went to town on those impressive side-burns and also chose to make more of Elvis' characteristic quiff. To balance the extra weight on top, I raised the height of the collar.

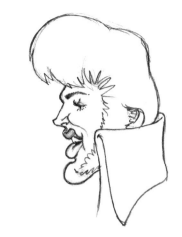

It's not looking too bad, but there's something a bit un-El-vissy about it, to my eye. The bigger lips have changed the overall shape of the lower face, making the chin seem weak. So maybe the solution would be to rein in the distortions a touch? Not likely. It's usually more successful to take things further. So with yet more layout paper, I did a new tracing of this caricature, this time enlarging the chin and bringing out the nose a touch further. I also made the quiff, sideburn and collar yet larger, moved the eye back further and enhanced the eye-lashes. That's better.

To add tone and shading, keep things really simple. If you have achieved a good likeness, don't muck it up with lots of unnecessary hatching. Do the minimum necessary to give the hair the right feel and then just add enough shading to the face to give it some weight and 'colour' in relation to the hair.

TIP: Don't try to enlarge every feature. In order for some parts to look big, other parts must be small. Be clear from the start what features you want to exaggerate and which to leave alone or diminish.

(021) Stir a Drink

There are fewer and fewer people taking sugar in their drinks these days, which means a growing ignorance of the need for decent stirring to dissolve it all. They think a cursory swirl of the spoon will suffice, leaving you with that last mouthful of syrupy sludge. And how often are you served tea in a cup and saucer with attendant teaspoon? Probably once a year at Auntie Flo's care home.

When someone has been kind enough to make you a cup of tea, it would seem ungrateful to send it back for a proper stir. So simply reach behind your ear for your trusty pencil and finish the job while no one's looking. Your tea will be properly stirred without causing offence to your host.

If tea is not the bag you're into, fear not—you will find that your pencil does an equally good job of stirring coffee. It also happens to be rather good for fishing out the tasty bits of foam from the dregs of a cappuccino.

(022) Draw with the Side of a Pencil

How do you hold a pencil? This may seem a silly question, but there are many possible answers. Your standard 'writing' grip will only get you so far in drawing. Changing how you hold your tool can open up new avenues to explore. For example, to map out rough guidelines many artists hold the pencil loosely between thumb and all four fingers, changing the way your whole arm moves and allowing for greater fluidity and gracefulness of line (see 054). For finely detailed work it is commonplace to hold the pencil almost vertical and very near the tip, allowing very fine control in delicate movements of the fingers. Experiment to find out what effects can work for you. Try sketching the same subject several times over with different grips.

One particularly useful grip holds the pencil almost horizontal to the paper so that you draw with the side edge of the graphite. For this you'll need to whittle a good length of graphite.

This technique allows you to fill in broad areas of tone, which can be quickly and quite smoothly applied, bringing a new dimension to quick sketches.

You can also complete entire drawings with the side edge of a pencil, producing interesting marks of varied thickness that can lend character to your drawing style and effortless texture to a subject.

 # Portage of Pants

No matter how firmly one undertakes to train offspring, spouses or flatmates, the problem will inevitably arise of randomly strewn undergarments on bedroom floors, under the sofa, halfway up the stairs and so on. It is a fact of life that others are not so scrupulous with the placement of such objects as your delicate self. Any item that has spent a day swaddling the sweaty parts of another is to be approached with caution and somehow transported to the laundry bin. In this task, the humble pencil may, once again, come to the rescue. The principle is simple: grasp your pencil—preferably one of full length—by the blunt end and insert the point firmly into the offending garment. With a deft upward turn, your pencil can be induced to raise the felonious item off the floor and hold it quite securely. Keeping your arm outstretched, proceed to the laundry bin, whereupon a dip of the wrist will allow the nasty article to fall harmlessly inside.

024 Bring a Drawing to Life

I suspect most readers will share my view that proper animation is something best left to other people. Very, very patient people. When it takes 24 painstaking drawings to create a single second of screen time, I am resigned that my 'Fantasia' will never come to light, not in this lifetime. But that doesn't mean that we can't put our pencils to the task of incredibly simple, yet surprisingly effective animation that requires only two, yes two, drawings.

Furnish yourself with a strip of paper, say 30 centimetres (12 inches) by 8 centimetres (3 inches), and fold it neatly in half. Open it up and on the inner surface do a little drawing. Think of something that would naturally move back and forth, like a dog with a wagging tail, a hen pecking or some blinking eyes, and draw that, with the moving part in one or other extreme of its movement. Then replace the top layer and carefully trace the drawing through—perhaps placing it on a window to help you see through (see 016). On the new picture, change the moving part to its opposite position.

The drawing is now finished, but you'll still need that pencil. Place it on the paper and roll the uppermost drawing tightly around it. Remove the pencil and let the paper unfurl.

The rolling is now finished, but you'll still need that pencil. Lay it back on top of the paper and move it rapidly back and forth. Thus the paper furls and flattens alternately, revealing the two drawings one after the other and making the picture appear to move.

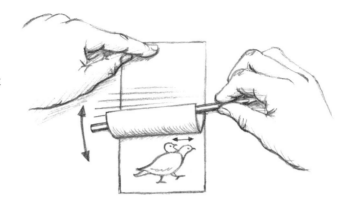

 # Noughts and Crosses

There was a time when every child learned the age-old game of noughts and crosses, but with the distractions of video games and DVDs perhaps this cunningly simple game has bypassed a generation or two, and may be worthy of resurrection.

All you need is a pencil or two, a scrap of paper and an opponent (preferably one slightly less devious than yourself). Draw a simple grid (see below) and the two players decide who will be noughts and who will be crosses. Taking turns, the players mark their symbol in any of the nine squares formed by the grid with the aim of placing three in a line—up, down or diagonally. Young minds will be enthralled by the many permutations of play.

However, the game can be easily engineered so that every time you get to go first you will always win: Instinctively, the novice aims to secure the middle square, but this is folly. Instead, place your first mark in a corner and wherever your opponent places their marks, aim for other corners. Once you have secured three corners, your opponent will be doomed. Try it. It really works.

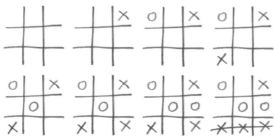

(026) Figure Drawing

As much as we like people, we have to admit they can be quite annoying at times. But in drawings they don't slurp their tea, pick their noses or leave their towels on the bathroom floor. With such power in your pencil, how could you resist drawing people (or 'figures' , as artists call them)? They can be tricky to draw, but they don't have to be. You need not struggle through life drawing classes . . . unless you live in a particularly liberated commune, it makes more sense to draw people with their kit on. Clothing hides a multitude of horrors and also makes the whole prospect far less daunting.

There is no reason to approach a figure drawing very differently to any other object. Look at the general masses and jot them down roughly. Make sure that all the parts of the body connect logically and check proportions here and there (see 052). Posture and proportion are the key elements to capturing the specific charms of an individual figure. For a seated figure, drawing the chair is not only nec-essary to stop them from appearing to hover, but it can also help to frame a figure and guide your drawing of it.

Once you have a solid framework established you can start to hone the outlines. Don't imagine that you know how a certain body part looks. Always refer closely to the model.

Switch to a softer pencil—nice and sharp—and set down definitive outlines. As you add the details of the clothing, draw the creases and folds of the fabrics: big fat folds for heavy garments, small multiple creases for thin fabric. Drawing the textures and the hang of the clothing goes a long way towards describing the figure inside. The style of the garments also says a lot about the person. A figure

drawing need not be thought of as a portrait, so you can keep the drawing of the face quite simple.

Sketching unsuspecting subjects can be particularly rewarding, capturing something of their natural behaviour. Choose slow-moving subjects: those sitting comfortably or immersed in an activity. A simple angle of view can help too, as with this nice old couple whom I observed having tea on a day trip. I have left all my mistakes and guidelines in place here and you can see the marks I made for their postures, the lady upright and the man slouching inside a gentle curve. The picnic table formed a helpful guide for placing and proportioning the figures relative to each other.

 ## 027 A Precise Pointer

Where would we be without our dexterous fingers and opposing thumbs? We tend to be quite pleased with the things that we can do with them. Useful though they are, they can sometimes let us down in pretty basic ways. If directing a stranger in the street, the finger does a creditable job in sending them in the right direction, but when pointing out a landmark on a map the same finger can prove woefully ambiguous. The same goes for drawing attention to a specific part of a text, photograph or diagram—'Do you mean the bit the fingertip is touching?' 'Oh, am I supposed to be looking beyond the end of the finger?' 'Are you pointing to the snotty kid in the middle row or the ugly one in the back row?'

It is the most natural thing to whip out your pencil and use the tip to indicate immediately and exactly, bypassing any possible confusion. We've all done it—perhaps that's why the tip of a pencil is called a 'point'.

The pencil also proves itself useful in many other functions of nimbleness. The tiny parts of a model aeroplane kit, sequins and spangles, fiddly screws from the back of a clock, can all be moved around and brought to order at the point of a pencil. You may find a small dead creature that is worthy of inspection. A pencil can turn it over and tease out all the little legs and mouthparts that could be crushed and spoilt by fumbling around with your sausage fingers. Speaking of which, there's a fair chance that your doctor's pencil has seen some action lifting certain body parts for visual inspection.

(028) Shading Patterns

One of the particular strengths of pencils in drawing is their facility for delicate shading, for building up subtle layers of tone to describe the fall of light and shade on a three-dimensional object. There are many different shading techniques or 'patterns', that may suit certain subjects or effects or may simply work better for different individuals.

Crosshatching is probably the most commonly used shading pattern. It starts by shading across broad areas with parallel straight lines. Successive changes of shading direction of your strokes build up the depths of tone for easily controllable layers.

There are many variants of this technique. Short strokes can be used to shade areas in small patches of overlapping crosshatching.

A more sophisticated form, favoured by rigorous academic draughtsmen, uses crisscrossing contour lines that wrap around a subject's form producing a particularly three-dimensional effect.

Hatching across an entire drawing in a single direction can look effective, but it can be tricky to pull off and tends to flatten the subject somewhat.

Subtle shading can be achieved by smudging the soft marks of the side of a pencil, although care must be taken to avoid everything getting quite messy.

A more controllable technique uses a blunted pencil to draw tiny swirling patterns repeatedly going over and over the surface.

There is nothing to stop you combining these techniques or coming up with your own methods. And then again, you could throw caution to the wind, wave your knickers in the air, and just scribble away merrily.

 # Circle and Centre Puzzle

This puzzle will really have everyone scratching their heads. How could you possibly draw a circle and a dot in the centre without taking your pencil off the paper? As you will have guessed, there's always a way for the devious at heart:

Here's the trick: Start by drawing a good firm dot in the middle of your paper. Keep the pencil in place and *fold the edge of the paper over* to meet the pencil. Then you can draw across the back of the paper away from the centre point before drawing back onto the front, unfolding the paper, and drawing the circle. Prepare for some groans and complaints. But you never said you couldn't draw on the back of the paper, did you?

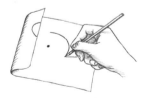

(030) Aerial Perspective

We go out to the countryside in search of quiet and fresh air. And 'this most excellent canopy the air' that invigorates the lungs feels good and pure and clean. But look into the distance. You see that line of trees on the horizon? They look kind of faint, don't they? That's because the air is not as pure as you think. It is a 'foul and pestilent congregation of vapours', dust, pollen, pollution and, even on a dry day, water vapour.

What this means to your drawing is that the further away something is, the more air you have to look through to see it, and this reduces tonal contrasts—an effect known as 'aerial perspective'. In pencil terms, objects that are close to you can be

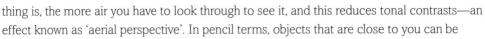

scribbled down with the full weight of a soft, black pencil, but those more distant will require a more subtle approach.

It makes sense to begin shading at the horizon, perhaps with a hard pencil, and work your way towards the foreground with increasingly strong pencil marks. It's not just the weight of pencil marks that captures the effects of aerial perspective; the size and quality of your marks count too, as well the brightness of the pale areas.

Aerial perspective can also be harnessed over much shorter distances. The effects may not be so very apparent to the eye, but you can impose them on a drawing to create a sense of distance between elements and give your drawings added depth and clarity. It's a bit of a fib, but not a bad one.

(031) Penetrate Cellophane

The modern age has given us washing machines, central heating, food processors and all manner of other devices to ease the burden of our physical existence. But progress gives with one hand and takes with the other—it has also brought shrink-wrap into our lives. I cannot tell you what purpose it serves to wrap household items in cellophane, but it is a fact of modern life that CDs, printer cartridges and the like cannot be accessed without somehow penetrating the outer layer. You can see the item, but you can't get at it. Opening a packet of biscuits can lead to frustrated picking at the end, searching in vain for a loose end to gain purchase. Even a cucumber resists ready consumption these days.

However, if you look behind your ear, you will find a ready tool to force your way inside. The pencil's point is strong enough to take advantage of any weakness in a cellophane barrier. Push the point into a seam and continue pushing at an acute angle, driving wedge-like into the wrapping until it splits. And once even a small split is made, the wrapping can be torn off with gay abandon. If you can't find a seam, use the pencil's point to 'draw' rapidly up and down along an indentation and the wrap will soon yield. Biscuits can be liberated by pushing the pencil into the side of the packet, between two biscuits. Similarly a vegetable's wrapping can be punctured straight through into the flesh, preferably at an end you don't intend to eat.

Don't forget that envelopes can be opened by pencil too. I know no one has used letter openers since Agatha Christie and a finger does the job perfectly well, but there is some pleasure to be had from using your pencil to open the morning's mail, albeit short-lived if the envelope contains a tax bill.

(032) Blunt Pencil Drawing

There is something quite gorgeous about a nice, sharp point on a pencil. Marks are clear and bold and precise and it just feels good. But have you noticed that a sharp pencil can actually inhibit your start on a drawing? It's maybe just too precise, too definitive. There is a lot to be said for starting off with a softer edge to your lines. Drawing with a well worn, rounded tip makes softer marks, which are more forgiving, making a drawing seem more approachable.

Sacrilegious though it may seem, the point of a pencil can be easily rounded off on a brick wall, sandpaper or even a bit scrap paper. If you're anything like me you'll already have a pot full of blunt pencils anyway. Ready? Now just draw something. There's no special technique to divulge here, just start off with the big masses and work your pencil around them, gradually honing details and letting the image appear out of your soft blunt marks. You will naturally respond by gradually building up the pressure as you become more confident of the developing form. The very act of drawing will build up layers of tone, as in this drawing of a deeply carved theatre mask.

Once a good drawing is established, it is perfectly valid to switch to a sharper pencil and define details further. Or you may prefer to stick with a less focused feel and finish the more detailed work with a softer, blunted pencil, as I did here. And, of course, you can also use an eraser to correct or soften any mistakes or lift out highlights.

033 Defuse a Mousetrap

They may appear cute and harmless, but once a resident rodent gets his tiny feet under your table it will not be long before you are overrun with the 'wee tim'rous beasties' weeing all over the vegetable rack. The setting of mousetraps must then be undertaken with a cold heart and an iron will. With careful placement (along a secluded skirting board) and the employment of effective bait (bits of Mars Bar are recommended) you can repose in the expectation of little snappings and squeakings going off while you enjoy the sleep of the righteous.

Those mousetraps that have failed in their murderous tasks by night, however, will need to be safely defused by day, lest any little fingers or wet noses find them. By far the safest way to defuse the lethal springs is to trigger them with the end of a pencil (assuming that your pencil is not whittled down to a stub). Hold the pencil loosely in preparation, for it to be whipped out of your grip in the customary somersault of the snapping device. For sport, see if you can beat the trap, releasing the spring and whisking the pencil away before it can be ensnared.

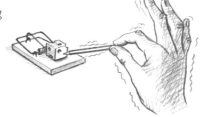

TIP: Whether you bait with cheese, raisins or chocolate, do not be tempted to have a nibble after use; it may very well be tainted with mouse wee.

034 Draw in Perspective

Perspective theory is often spoken of in hushed tones, like mystical truths—the secrets of the ancients. In one way this is true: the art of perspective, practiced in the classical world, was lost in the gloom of the Dark Ages (which is why a lot of medieval art looks a bit naive to our modern eyes) and only rediscovered in the fifteenth century. Then it sparked the rebirth or 'Renaissance' of classical ideals, and some clever bods got rather good at art. But, elusive though it was for so many centuries, perspective is actually quite easy to grasp and fun to play around with. Here we'll look at the simplest form, known as 'one-point perspective'. (For 'two-point' perspective see 048.)

It all starts with the horizon: a perfectly horizontal line that stands for the viewer's eye-level. Somewhere along that line will be a single 'vanishing point' (hence 'one-point' perspective), the fixed position of the viewer's eye at which all receding lines converge. For this demonstration we'll plonk the vanishing point in the middle of the horizon, so draw a horizontal line and mark the middle. Then, using a ruler draw a number of straight lines converging on your vanishing point. Use very light pencil marks (not like the clunking heavyweight lines I've drawn here, for clarity).

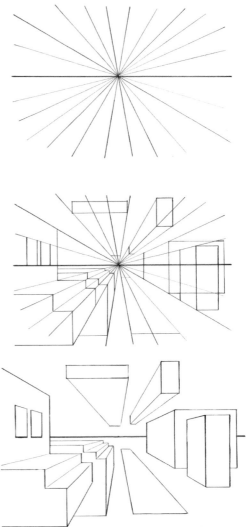

In one-point perspective, all horizontals, other than those that recede away from view should be drawn strictly horizontal. And all vertical lines remain strictly vertical. So you can start to develop an imaginative drawing by ruling horizontal and vertical lines quite arbitrarily amongst your network of receding lines.

To bring clarity to your constructions, erase any now redundant perspective lines. Thus you are left with a set of solid looking blocks that occupy a believable looking space. You can see that where lines recede downwards to the horizon they seem to sit above you and those that recede upwards appear to be looked down upon. Feel free to add further details, shading or develop your imaginative scene as you see fit. The important thing here is to get a feel for how an understanding of perspective makes simple sense of an otherwise confusing a mass of receding lines.

Once these principles are lodged in your brain you can get out in the real world and use them to bring some order to your drawings of interiors and street scenes. The important thing is to identify the horizon and vanishing point, which may require some initial assessment of receding angles (see 060). You will soon develop the confidence to draw any necessary perspective guidelines free-hand, as I did for this sketch.

TIP: You will rarely be able to see the actual horizon, but you can work out its level by observation. Just look for lines of brickwork, windowsills, fireplaces that appear level to your eye.

(035) Create an Impression

Let me tell you a true story. There was once a struggling young bachelor who traipsed the streets of London, portfolio in hand, showing his illustration samples to any publishing employee bored enough give him a few minutes of their time. One particular lady editor had the great wisdom to give this young man a commission. Some weeks later, once the job was done, she asked him out on a date. Very soon a romance blossomed. But what had this successful editor seen in the penniless illustrator? Other than his staggering good looks and radiant charisma, the most potent impression that lasted with the lady was the end of a pencil sticking out of the illustrator's hankie pocket. That young man, I confess, was me and the editor is now my wife. And a lovely thing she is too.

You would have to be quite a dandy to wander around with a silken triangle sticking out of your breast pocket these days, and such pockets go largely unused. What a wasted opportunity. Show yourself to be all arty and intellectual and simultaneously a serious-minded man of action. All it takes is a pencil. But the pencil must be a long one, else it will not be visible above the pocket top. And be warned: a pencil short enough to be obscured from view is a pencil short enough to fall horizontal in the pocket and result in much undignified fishing around when its inevitable need arises, which may result in the very opposite of the effect you're after.

Draw Dramatic Light

As we have seen, the pencil cannot draw light. It can only suggest its presence by drawing the areas of shade that light cannot reach. Light, in a drawing, is the white of the paper. Drawings of light and shade can be complex, subtle and atmospheric. . . but hey, let's not concern ourselves with subtlety! A simplified approach can actually be rather more dramatic.

A single, bright, direct light source, such as a desk lamp or sunlight makes for strong contrasts between the light and dark parts of a subject. Dark, featureless areas of shadow are easier to see and draw than the subtle nuances

of shade, or 'tone' created by diffused or multiple light sources. This rocking horse was lit in such a way so that I could treat all the shaded areas with the same heavy tone of a very soft pencil (6B) and leave all the light parts as pure white paper. The only real concession I made to shades of grey ('mid tones') was in the transitions from dark to light, which I blended to show the roundedness of the horse's form.

Crafty old masters like Caravaggio and Rembrandt developed a distinctive style known as chiaroscuro ('light-dark' in Italian), characterised by brightly lit subjects disappearing into featureless, black shadow, making the light seem all the more bright (and meaning that you can get away with drawing only half the subject).

Here's my rocking horse again with the background filled in with solid black. You can see how much more brightly the white shines and that the details on the darker side of the horse disappear entirely into the background.

A similar effect of inverse silhouette is achieved when a subject is placed against a naturally occurring dark background. The sunlight on this cottage appears all the brighter for being framed against a growth of dark trees. Deep shadows under the eaves also contrast with the white of the paper, adding to the effect of bright sunlight.

Dramatic lighting effects always arise when you place yourself looking towards a strong light source, such as I did in drawing this factory unit. Again the tonal variations are naturally reduced and could be captured adequately with two basic shades of grey. In drawings like this, the subject is really the arrangement of light and shadow rather than the buildings and shrubs.

(037) The Bendy Pencil Illusion

With no practice at all you can make a pencil, which we all know to be a rigid object, appear to bend as if made of rubber.

You may allow any viewers to inspect the pencil first and prime them with a suitably grandiose statement, like 'Behold my awesome powers! Solid wood turns to rubber under my magical grasp!' Hold the end of your pencil very loosely, twixt thumb and forefinger, then oscillate your hand quickly so that the pencil wobbles up and down, just a couple of centimetres at first. Gradually increase the amount of wobble, saying 'I can feel it melting!' It really looks bendy, doesn't it?

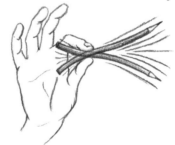

I don't know why this trick works. It just does. Let's not spoil the magic for ourselves.

(038) Draw Plants

Tricky things, plants. Don't get me wrong, they're very nice and everything, but can be quite devilishly tricky to draw. The trouble is they have so many bits, all jostling around and vying for sunlight. Ah, but there may be a plan behind all the chaos, an orderly geometric structure. Work that out and you're half way there.

Before drawing this potted sunflower I had a good long look at it and worked out that the leaves spiral around a central stem, getting progressively smaller towards the top—so far so good. Furthermore, they grow out at regular intervals, which make them seem to fit into clear squares and triangles. Maybe this is just me imposing my will on the plant, but even so, recognising such structures and drawing them as rough guidelines brings a very helpful sense of order to the subject.

Within my rough grid I could easily draught the general

shapes, sizes and placements of the leaves. I also worked on the flower, not observing individual petals closely, but indicating their general forms.After a bit of cleaning up with an eraser, I drew the petals in more detail and approximated the serrations of the leaves' outlines.

My aim with the shading was to bring further clarity to the subject, to use the light and shadows falling on the plant to make the structure clearly visible. Dark shadows also bring some form to the central area, the inner parts of the plant, giving the drawing depth. In reality, the leaves are very dark in tone, but to shade them thus would make the whole drawing very heavy and muddy.

Flora of this world are as varied as the ways of drawing them. Different plants will naturally call for different approaches. A ragged sun-drenched palm was crying out for a vigorous drawing style, this time eschewing any attempt at order and aiming instead to depict the jumbled mass of jagged outlines. Maybe you'll draw a whole load of different plants in a scene. Here it would perhaps be more appropriate to treat each plant as a general mass and aim for distinctive overall shapes and textures.

(039) Ceiling Darts

Let's be honest, working in an office really cannot match the discomforts, dangers and stresses of more manly jobs. Nevertheless, it can have a cumulative dulling, de-humanising effect on the individual. In such cases, it can do wonders for the morale to perform minor acts of transgression—like spearing the ceiling with pencils.

Sharpen your pencil to a fine point, preferably using a knife to whittle a good length of lead. Take the pencil by the blunt end. Push back in your chair to give yourself some clearance from the desk and flick the pencil up in the air as hard as you can. The aim is to get it to stick into the soft fibreboard of a suspended ceiling. This takes a wee bit of practice to perform successfully, but much of the fun is to be had from the challenge and the sense of achievement when you eventually pull it off.

If your office ceiling is made of sterner stuff than fibreboard, never fear, because there is another way. Plunder the stationary cupboard for a stick of glue and get a goodly gob of the stuff on the blunt end of your pencil. Then cast it upwards in the aforementioned fashion.

Best to practice when you're working late and have the office to yourself. Once you have achieved a good average, practice doing it as casually as you can, so that the act and effort of throwing would be barely noticeable to onlookers. From then, you can amuse yourself by darting the ceiling amid the throng of a busy day and commit this minor vandalism without detection. Or why not challenge your workmates to contests? You could leave the pencils in place as trophies of your skill—or hanging like Swords of Damocles over your career.

(040) Motion Lines

The world of cartoons has given us a rich visual language that is immediately accessible to all. Even small children can understand the shorthand of motion lines that lend cartoon figures illusions of speed, shakiness, levitation and so on. They are simple to employ, immediately effective and often quite amusing.

Here is a little poppet shown without any cartoon effects. She looks jolly enough, but fairly static.

With various styles of motion lines added we can read the figure in lots of different ways and delight in the playfulness of the cartoon language. In most cases the basic figure remains entirely unchanged throughout, although effects can be heightened with small changes to facial expression or body language. The secret is to keep the marks minimal and decisive and to avoid mixing up too many different types of motion lines in the same drawing.

You'll see that motion lines give you quite a useful set of tools to influence the reading of an image, and it can be fun to play around with these tools outside the field of cartooning. A few strokes of the pencil can add an extra dimension to many 'serious' drawings. You can deface pictures in books, newspapers or management handouts with actions or emotions quite unintended by the original image-makers. There is no surer way to puncture pomposity.

041 Lubricate a Lock

Aside from its marvellous mark-making capabilities, graphite (the grey stuff inside your pencil) has other useful qualities. One of these is lubrication. If you have a door that needs some persuasion to close properly, take a soft pencil (4B or similar) and scribble vigorously on the curved edge of the door's latch bolt (that's the metal bit that protrudes out of the door's edge). The latch bolt will now slide with miraculous ease and the door will shut without any slamming required.

If the internal workings of a lock are stiff or frozen, rub your pencil along both sides of the key, push it in and out of the lock and wiggle it around. Repeat the process if necessary and soon the lock will turn like a dream. This principle can be equally useful on sticky hinges, curtain rods, drawer runners and many other surfaces that need to slide against each other.

042 Draw Animals

Everyone likes animals. Maybe not so much when they're nesting in your loft, humping your leg or threatening to tear chunks out of you, but generally, we think they're nice. So it follows that they should make good drawing subjects, if only the little blighters would co-operate. Even docile creatures have annoying tendencies to turn away, roam around or sniff each other's bums as soon as you get your pencils out. So you'll need some patience to sketch animals successfully. A few hard-won tips can help too.

The first thing to take on board is that sketches of animals will often have to be based on just a few mere glances. Unless you have all the time in the world, it is therefore unwise to aim for a high level of finish. Instead, go for a lively sketching style and make lots of quick sketches, rather than wasting a lot of time waiting for a creature to resume a former position.

One way to keep animals from moving away is to shove some food under their noses. They quite like food. Mind you, even when they remain on the spot, they move constantly. However, you too can move. To draw this giraffe the zoo's viewing platform gave me a lovely perspective, and because I was on my feet, I could move around to follow the shuffling of the giraffe.

Zoo animals tend to be quite bored and, having nothing better to do, will often sit still for long periods. That was the case with this crocodile, but whilst he remained motionless for several minutes, a succession of zoo visitors were not so accommodating and did their very best to obscure my view or lure the croc's attention elsewhere.

A really useful trick for drawing animals is to work on multiple sketches at the same time, on the same sheet. As a creature shifts position start another drawing and then return to previous views as the animal resumes earlier poses. It is even easier if you work with a group of animals. When drawing these lazy cows, I was able to observe similar views of different individuals and piece together the various body parts.

Pets have your trust and allow you to get really close. Bribe them with food or ask a nice person to shower them with attention. It is relatively easy to draw them when sleeping, but still they twitch and fidget. At least my little spaniel does, as she dreams of chasing rabbits through verdant, sunlit meadows.

Many regional museums have collections of stuffed animals. Sometimes the taxidermy leaves much to be desired, but other examples offer wonderful opportunities to observe splendid beasts in naturalistic and dynamic poses … and presenting opportunites for interesting or unusual viewpoints. Take as much time as you like. Go and have a cup of tea; he'll still be there when you come back.

(043) House Puzzle

This is an old one. You may have seen it before, but do you remember the solution? Pay attention this time and get it into your head so that you can prove your superiority over challengees. All you have to do is draw this simple figure without taking the pencil off the page or going over the same line twice.

There are two possible solutions involving no clever tricks: it is just a case of starting at the correct point and drawing the lines in the right order. Start in a bottom corner and follow one of these diagrams. Once you've done it a couple of times, it will seem obvious.

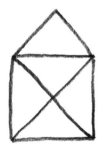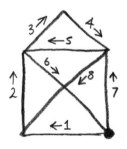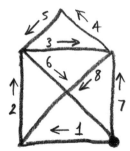

Caricature Sketching

A drawing is not a photograph and cannot capture every tiny detail with perfect precision. So, in a way, all drawing is caricature, whether or not the subject is conspicuously distilled. In portraiture, certain features will often be subtly emphasised to bring about an enhanced likeness or characterisation. Indeed, artists such as Gainsborough and Sargent were sought after for their skills in bringing out the more flattering aspects of a sitter—a subtle form of caricature (and nice work if you can get it).

A drawing is not a photograph and cannot capture every tiny detail with perfect precision. So, in a way, all drawing is caricature, whether or not the subject is conspicuously distilled. In portraiture, certain features will often be subtly emphasised to bring about an enhanced likeness or characterisation. Indeed, artists such as Gainsborough and Sargent were sought after for their skills in bringing out the more flattering aspects of a sitter—a subtle form of caricature (and nice work if you can get it).

We can learn much from the masters and working from their portrait paintings makes for great practice at caricaturing—much of the work having been done already. It is also much easier to draw from a flat image than a real person.

Start by identifying the most noticeable feature, maybe the nose, mouth or face shape and draw it BIG. Then look for the more diminutive features and draw them extra small. Fit the other features in amongst them and consider enlarging or reducing the spaces in between. Maintain an air of impish disrespect throughout.

TIP: However grotesquely you may exaggerate other features draw the eyes carefully and naturalistically. The eyes contain much of a portrait's character and attitude so, unless they are particularly striking, it's best not to fool around with them.

Do lots of such sketches, allowing just a few minutes for each. Before long you may even find that some likenesses come naturally. If not, you will still have achieved some weird and characterful faces and gained some painless practice of facial features that will prove invaluable in drawing 'serious' portraits. Here are some of the dozens of five-minute caricature sketches I have made to amuse myself in stately homes and art museums.

(045) Reveal a Hidden Message

Here's one for amateur sleuths. Imagine this scenario: a suspect is under surveillance and you observe them taking a serious phone call and jotting something down on a notepad. They tear off the note and take it away with them. The contents of that note may be the vital evidence you need to prove their involvement with an international diamond smuggling ring. If only you could see the note's contents. Picking their pocket would be much too dangerous, but get hold of the notepad and you're in with a chance. You'll need a soft pencil with a good length of lead. Hold it almost flat against the surface of the note-  pad's top sheet and gently rub the pencil in broad strokes across the whole surface. The impression left behind by the original note will be instantly revealed, incriminating the ne'er-do-well and lining you up for a citizens' award.

Of course you needn't be a sleuth to benefit from this technique; it is equally useful for the mistrustful spouse, the concerned parent and the good old Nosey Parker. But it's worth bearing in mind that you're likely to reveal nothing juicier than a shopping list.

Compositional Thumbnails

When we admire a piece of music it is more than the mere notes that moves us, but also the spaces between the notes, the stresses and sustains, harmonies, countermelodies and so on. A conductor has a baton; an artist has a pencil. Of all the principles of drawing, few are more essential than composition—the arrangement of elements within the boundaries or 'frame' of a picture. A skilfully executed drawing badly composed will always look weak, whereas a strong composition will shine through a very simple sketch, or even one quite badly drawn. All can be worked out with just a few strokes of a pencil. And a few basic principles won't do any harm.

As a billion amateur snapshots prove, the most tedious way to compose a picture is to plonk the main subject slap bang in the middle surrounded by dead space.

By moving the horizon up or down it immediately divides a picture into more interesting, uneven spaces. Placing the subject off-centre has a similar effect. Since ancient times, artists and architects have relied heavily on a formula known as the 'golden section'—a mathematically calculated ideal division of a space. We can ignore the maths and think of it as a 'rule of thirds', diving the frame into roughly a third and two thirds upwards and across.

  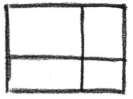

The size of a main subject within the frame makes a big difference to how it feels in the picture. Making the subject small diminishes its presence in the picture and gives more weight to the surroundings. Or you can choose to fill the frame with your subject, creating a more intense focus or claustrophobic effect.

Bringing in surrounding features also affects a composition. Lines running though a composition lead the eye into or around a picture, Looking past or through foreground features creates a kind of 'frame within a frame' that also has the effect of drawing the eye in.

Artists and illustrators typically produce many tiny 'thumbnail' sketches to try out compositions before spending lots of time on a drawing. Here are some thumbnails I drew whilst roaming around an impressive ruin. As well as interesting arrangements of shapes, I was looking for tonal balance—a pleasing arrangement of light and dark on the page. I used a soft pencil to sketch basic grey silhouettes and then used it more heavily for a second, darker tone. A couple of tones are enough for you to tell if a composition is likely to succeed or not.

TIP: Composition offers vast and fascinating possibilities, far beyond the scope of this brief introduction. Look at drawings, paintings and photographs in galleries and books and analyse the compositions and how your eye is led around the surface.

(047) Write a Bestseller

Nobel Prize winner, John Steinbeck, wrote many great classics of American literature with a pencil. Roald Dahl had a whole pot of them, which he worked his way through during each day to avoid interrupting his flow of creative juices with tiresome sharpening. Vladimir Nabokov, Truman Capote, Earnest Hemingway and others all famously wrote in pencil.

You have at your fingertips the very same technology as those literary giants, so what is to stop you from becoming the next J. K. Rowling? Better get on with it then.

First your need a premise, or 'set up', if you like. Make it completely original and intriguing. Make it rich in possibilities for romance, adventure, sidesplitting comedy and gravitas. Gravitas is good. Publishers like gravitas. Now decide on a setting: historical, pastoral, exotic, poverty stricken, desolate, fantastical, futuristic, or maybe you could mix them all up in an epic saga that defies the logic of time and space. Got that? Good.

A story must be populated. Women spend a lot more money on books than men, so go for a female protagonist. She must be beautiful, obviously, and strong, but also a little vulnerable. Give her a woeful back-story—maybe school bullying or a distant and controlling father figure—and she'll need a love interest or several. The men should be variously butch, handsome, rich, sensitive, righteous and poor. Make sure she ends up with the poor one. The villain of the piece need not be an embodiment of pure unrelenting evil, although that's never a bad thing, but he/she/it must be magnificently memorable. If his/her/its name should go on to enter common usage, so much the better.

Get things underway with a powerful and quotable opening line that leads into a nice cosy set up with all things rubbing along swimmingly. Then upset the apple cart with a weird and intriguing event that will give your heroine a something to do for the following 400 pages. By the end, all problems should be resolved, involv- ing at least one unlikely coincidence, and your heroine will have learned something profound in the process.

I think that covers everything. Off you go then, and don't come back until you've got 150,000 words of pure gold. And don't forget to cut me in. A small percentage, say 2 or 3 per cent, will suffice.

(048) Two-point Perspective

Q: What makes more noise than a pig stuck under a gate?
A: Two pigs stuck under a gate.
Just as our earlier exercise in one-point perspective provides a simple system for bringing order to a confusing array of angles, working with two-point perspective yields yet more answers.

Most of us have some grasp of this principle already. If I asked you to draw a box you'd probably come up with something like this without having to think about it.

Now we can apply some rules to this principle and extend your drawing range. Draw such a box in the middle of a large sheet of paper and then, with a ruler extend the receding lines until they meet at either side. Between these two meeting points rule a horizontal line (it may need some adjustments to make it all work neatly). So now you have your eye-level, or 'horizon', and two vanishing points for an exercise in two-point perspective.

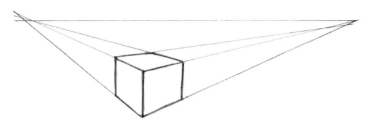

With this system, all uprights remain truly vertical. To get things underway draw a series of vertical lines arbitrarily around the page. Then rule them off to either vanishing point. It should already look like a three-dimensional space is emerging.

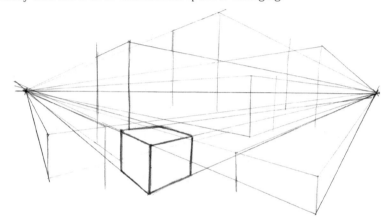

Now erase unneeded guidelines and strengthen the drawing around the shapes you have created. As we saw with one-point perspective (034), perspective theory makes it quite easy to draw an imaginary construction that works in convincing perspective.

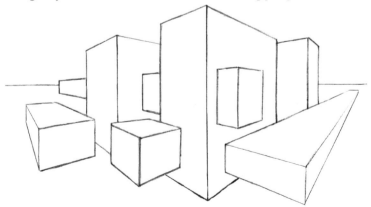

Drawing real scenes or objects you will probably find that vanishing points fall a long way off the edge of your page, making it totally impractical to rule to them accurately. No matter, you should be able to assess the main angles by eye (or with your pencil, 060). With just a few angles in place you can easily construct a kind of grid to work within and guide the rest of the drawing.

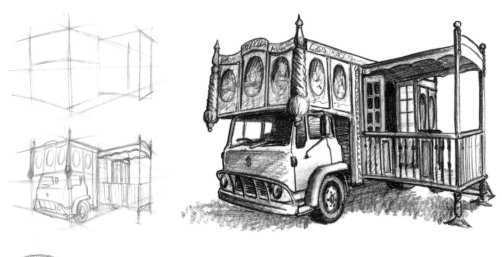

(049) A Toy for a Cat

For some reason, cats find the size and shape of a pencil eternally interesting. Seeing as they like pencils so much, why not let them have their fun? Just be careful not to let them play with any pencils that are very sharp, or any that have a rubber on the end, in case they chew it off and swallow it.

And you can make a pencil yet more intriguing for a cat. Sharpen both ends and blunt the tips by rubbing them on a brick wall or any rough surface. Then put the toy on the floor in front of your cat and push down one of the tips to make the other end rise. Put the cat's paw on the end and show her how to do it for herself. She'll soon get the hang of it and you can sit back and watch her amuse herself for hours, simple soul that she is.

Vigorous Drawing

There is much to be said for thoughtful drawing, well proportioned and sensitively shaded. There is also much to be said for scribbling away with gay abandon. Some subjects naturally lend themselves to the latter approach. Here, for example, is a sketch of a bust of some old pope or bishop or something. His face is craggy, lop-sided and really old (look at the size of his ears!), so there's no need to aim for beauty. In fact, the rough, spontaneous marks only add to his careworn character.

Similarly, a rustic stile in a winter landscape is intrinsically scrappy looking and demands an appropriately vigorous drawing approach. After roughly setting down the composition and perspective with an HB pencil I sketched the details of the horizon before getting out a softer pencil. With all the hard work done, and my fingers starting to get cold, I could then attack the paper with woody, branchy, earthy and weed-like marks and completed the drawing in a satisfying few minutes. I then put my gloves back on and went off to find a cup of tea to warm my fingers around.

(051) Fix Your Hair Up

This is a handy trick for ladies with long hair. Or men. Men can have long hair too. Your pencil can get your hair up off your swan-like neck and safely out of the way of dangerous machinery. This trick may seem like a bit of a faff, but I am reliably informed that it's very easy to master and can then be performed in mere seconds.

1.   Form a high ponytail with the left hand and, with the right hand, place the pencil above it, close to the head.
2.   Holding the pencil firmly, lift the ponytail and bring it over the top of the pencil. Wrap it round two or three times, depending on the length of your hair.
3.   Holding your hair in place with the left hand, rotate the end of the pencil downwards through 90 degrees, so that the pencil points upwards.
4.   Now the tricky bit: Lift the back of the pencil up through 180 degrees, so that the point is now facing downwards.
5.   Push the pencil down through the hair until the point protrudes near the bottom.

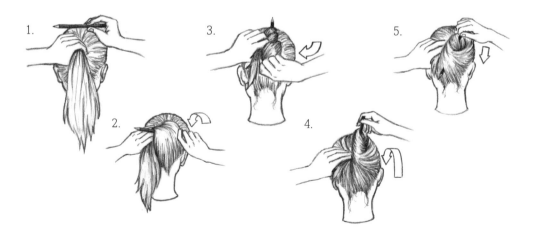

Et voila! Let go and your hair will remain miraculously in place. Go to the mirror and admire your new chic and bohemian look. Parade around the streets confident in the knowledge that you're looking good and also have an extra, emergency pencil to hand.

TIP: Do not create this hairstyle too low on the back of the head. A sudden glance upwards could leave you with a puncture wound in the back of the neck.

(052) Sight Sizing

It is an unwritten rule that an artist in a movie must be shown squinting intently at a pencil in his or her outstretched hand. What, I hear you ask, is all that about? Beyond being Hollywood's lazy shorthand for an 'artist', it's actually a very useful trick for measuring and checking proportions within a drawing.

With your arm held straight out in front of you and the elbow locked, you can take a measurement of a part of a subject by marking the length it appears to be, with your thumb against the pencil. In drawing this old house, for example, I found that my pencil measurement for the length of the chimney was repeated in other parts of the house, which greatly helped me to draw the rough construction lines. To ascertain the width of the gate, I measured it with my pencil and then found another similar proportion on the house, the height of the gable and top post. As long as you and your subject do not move around, and you always keep your elbow locked straight, the pencil will always be a consistent distance between your eye and your subject, and therefore a constant measure you can return to throughout the drawing.

TIP: You may be tempted to use this device to constantly check and recheck every proportion, but this is no surer way to crush any spontaneity and joy in the drawing process. Once you're reasonably happy with the proportions, get on with drawing freely and with spirit.

053 Make an Electrical Circuit

Here's a bit of fun masquerading as a science project. You can use a pencil to literally draw a working electrical circuit on a piece of paper. Make sure it's a very soft pencil and scribble a line—straight, wobbly, Mickey Mouse shaped—it doesn't matter, so long as you make the line very thick and heavy, going over it several times to get lots of graphite onto the paper.

Use crocodile clips or sticky tape to fix a short length of wire between one end of your circuit and one terminal of a 9V battery. Then attach a wire between the other battery terminal and a small light bulb or LED, and attach a third wire to the remaining light bulb terminal. All right so far?

Now press the spare end of wire onto your pencil line and 'Bingo!' the bulb will light up. Dimly. But as you move the wire along your pencil line, the light will brighten. Oooooh...

Now for the science bit: graphite is a conductor, but a very poor one, so the less graphite the current has to pass through, the less resistance it meets and the stronger the flow of electricity. It acts like a dimmer switch. Graphite is used in the manufacture of electrical resistors and is also poised to revolutionise the computer industry in the next generation of microcircuits.

054 Draw with Your Shoulder

For small-scale drawing, it probably feels natural to hold your pencil in a 'scribe's grip', as you would when writing. But that can be really quite inhibiting. Such a grip requires that the arm be supported, usually by resting on the desktop or drawing board. So the marks you make will be constrained by the arc of the pencil's movement from the wrist or elbow. Try this test: hold the pencil in your writing grip and draw a straight line right across a sheep of paper. As you progress the line becomes stilted and hesitant. Now change your grip and hold the pencil loosely between thumb and all four fingers. Lift your arm off the table and draw another straight line, this time making the movement from the shoulder. You should be able to whip across the page in a smooth even stroke.

Most of the drawings done for this small book have been done necessarily small. But I have utilised a range of grips throughout, only slipping back to the scribes grip occasionally. Even small drawings can benefit from the freedom of movement that comes from the shoulder. It is especially useful for mapping out rough guidelines and for energetic sketches and shading. To get yourself into the habit, have a go at a larger-scale drawing on an upright surface. If you don't happen to have an easel kicking around (well, why would you?), fix some paper to a wall or door. Make it high enough that you can reach the whole surface without having to bend down.

Your choice of subject is not too important, but perhaps it's best to avoid anything too precise or pretty (advice I have clearly ignored in doing a self-portrait). I did this at A2 (42cm x 60cm). The larger scale and upright positioning force you to work from

the shoulder and adapt your pencil grip. As you get into such a drawing you will probably start holding the pencil in various ways to approach the paper from the necessary angle or with the necessary weight. I often find myself using a very firm grip with the end of the pencil pushed into the palm, allowing me to put a lot of force behind my marks.

The result may not be the most polished work you have ever done, but it will probably have a loose and energetic feel that may have previously eluded you. Hopefully, you will also enjoy the process and be encouraged to make regular forays out of your comfort zone and start using your pencil not like a mere scribe, but like an *artist*.

(055) Spin the Pencil

This is very much like the old party game of 'Spin the Bottle'. Actually it's almost exactly the same. Invite your best-looking friends, ideally plied with alcohol, to sit around a bare table. Place a single pencil in the middle of the table and take it turns to spin the pencil with all your might. Each time the pencil comes to rest, whomsoever it points to must perform a forfeit, previously agreed, with the spinner.

A spinning pencil comes to rest very quickly. It is effectively random in its pointing direction, but perhaps a longer spinning time would increase tension around the table. To make it rotate at a more leisurely pace, push a drawing pin or thumb tack into the side of the pencil at the mid point (it may need some adjustment to achieve perfect balance). Then spin the pencil on the pin.

I'll leave it to your level of degradation/powers of persuasion to determine the nature and degree of the forfeits.

(056) Anthropomorphism

The dictionary informs me that this unwieldy word means 'the attribution of human motivation, characteristics or behaviour to inanimate objects, animals, or natural phenomena'. So there you are: anthropomorphism is about making things that are not people look a bit like people.

Everyone loves a cartoon: talking trains, singing, dancing crockery, extreme violence among domestic animals. It's no challenge to take any object and simply draw a face on it. And there you have a chirpy character.

But the concept of anthropomorphism has many further possibilities. It is more challenging and satisfying to work with the characteristics of a subject and accentuate human characteristics that already exist. This car, for example, viewed from the correct angle, has a very human face. There is not one line on this drawing that was not present on the real car. But by applying extra pressure to the pencil as I drew certain lines, and by leaving out distracting details, a distinctly human character emerges.

You can do the same with an animal very easily. Merely turning up the corners of an animal's mouth will give it an smile that readily translates as a cheerfully human nature and makes the subject all the more endearing. You can draw clothing on a creature or pose it in a human action and create an impression of intelligent activity without having to subject the creature to the full Disney treatment.

There is further fun to be had from turning the concept on its head and giving a person the characteristics of an animal. Here, Harry Potter is caricatured to look a bit like an owl, drawing on the actor's facial features, the character's glasses and the bird he keeps as a pet.

TIP: Unless you are particularly interested in cartooning, anthropomorphism is usually most effective when applied more subtly than in these examples. With a light touch, it can draw unconscious emotional responses from the viewer that are more powerful than when they are 'in on the joke'.

(057) Relieve Delicate Itches

I once had an operation on my right wrist (yes, I heard all the jokes.) My arm was encased in plaster and I was unable to work for six glorious weeks. Nevertheless, I soon started carrying a pencil around with me. As dead skin flaked off into my festering cast it became intolerably itchy. Everyone told me to scratch it with knitting needle. Now, you can't wander around town with a knitting needle in your top pocket, but a pencil is quite acceptable. Working from both ends of the cast with the full length of the pencil I was able to reach any problem area and bring instant, delirious relief.

Now, it's thankfully rare that I have to wear a plaster cast, but I do wear shoes quite a lot. I'm funny like that. An itch on the foot can be quite impossible to ignore, but what are you to do in public? Take your shoe off on a crowded train? No one wants that. With deft manoeuvring, all but the ends of the toes can be reached with a good length of pencil and a good length of satisfaction achieved.

Any doctor will tell you that the only object you should ever insert into your ears is your elbow. Sound advice from a medical point of view, but it fails to take account of the sensual pleasure that can be derived from a delicate probing of aforementioned orifices.

Before attempting this, make sure that there is no threat of being nudged by work colleagues or jumped upon by small children. And most vitally, always use the blunt end of the pencil. Not the pointy end. NEVER THE POINTY END! Then you should be safe to have a gentle rummage, scratch that itch and sink into cross-eyed ecstasy. Do not be tempted to probe too deeply; you don't want to be wiping off chunks of brain with the earwax.

(058) Draw Pretty Landscapes

I have a difficult confession to make: when it comes to drawing cheery pastoral landscapes, the type we enjoy looking at, pencil may not be the ideal medium. There, I've said it. Trees are usually quite dark in tone, clear skies are subtle and flawless, clouds extremely bright and fluffy, differing foliage, so distinctive in colour, can be tonally very similar. Attempting to render a pretty landscape in pencil can produce a heavy, clumsy, somewhat illegible drawing.

So, we have to be inventive, take control of the situation and apply a considered drawing language to the task in hand. As is often the case, 'less is more'—it's what we leave out that makes the difference.

Most importantly, establish a pleasing composition, then if the drawing gets too heavy you've still got a satisfying arrangement of shapes on the page (see 046). Unless you want to make a specific feature of cloud formations, leave the sky pure white. Now ignore local tones, pretend you can't see the inherent darkness of the grass and foliage, and concentrate instead on areas of shadow. Taking this little sketch as an example, the tree is shaded on its dark under parts, but where it is lit by the sun I have left it largely white. We know than trees are not white, but we also know their shape and that alone is enough to inform the viewer. Likewise, the gate here was not white, but to make it stand out clearly against the hedge behind I left it unshaded, like a silhouette in reverse.

Employ different types of mark to distinguish between various types of foliage and ground textures. The aim is to make the landscape appear varied and legible, even if you have to cheat a little by drawing things more varied than they really appear. Aerial perspective is also a useful tool for forcing a separation between areas of a picture, getting progressively fainter into the far distance (see 030).

Keep broad areas of shading to a minimum. Here the shading merely describes the flat tone of the grass, and acts as a contrast to the brightness of the rocks and cliffs. The few trees and bushes can here be shaded in their natural tone because they are of distinctive shape and small enough not to overwhelm the picture.

(059) Newspaper Graffiti

Graphite works well on newspaper paper. At art school, we got through great drums of the stuff, expressing our tortured souls. In the grown-up world the application of pencil on newspaper is more refined. Crosswords, Sudokus, word searches and all the other diverting fancies of the puzzle pages are best tackled with a pencil. Ideally one with a rubber on the other end, ideally. It's so much more genteel to erase a mistake than to go over it in progressively heavier biro marks.

And there is more, so much more, fun to be had with a newspaper and pencil. Seek out photographs of particularly odious politicians or celebrities of the week and augment them with your own satirical statements in the form of ridiculous moustaches. There are many styles of moustache and they are all ridiculous. You have the barely visible and appropriately named 'Pencil' moustache of the matinee idol, the 'Toothbrush' or 'Charlie Chaplin' moustache, the 'Handlebar' favoured by the flamboyant gentleman, the 'Horseshoe', the 'Dali', the 'Soup Strainer', the 'Painter's Brush', the 'Sergeant Major', the 'Fu Manchu' and so on. Each moustache has it's own social connotations that you can exploit to powerful effect—or just plain silliness. And then there are sideburns, and beards, and hairstyles, fangs, scars, spectacles . . . in fact there is no limit to the potential range of creative modifications to which you can subject your targets. With practice you can carefully match the weight of your marks with the density of ink and make quite lifelike additions. It's all good, clean, harmless fun, without any resort to genitalia.

 060 Assessing Angles

Because we think we know what things look like, it is often difficult to override our expectations when we come to draw them. Take a simple building, for example. We know that the roof, gutters, window line and so on are horizontal. Even when we understand the principles of perspective (see 034 and 048) our brains often refuse to acknowledge how steeply these lines can recede when seen at an angle.

Your pencil can be really helpful for making quick assessments of the receding angles in a subject, to get a drawing off to a confident start. Close one eye and hold your pencil upright in front of you. Tilt it left or right until it lines up with the relevant part of your subject. (Do not let it tip forward or backward.) With the angle established, bring your hand down to your paper to show you how the line should appear on your drawing.

This device is also useful for drawing all sorts of subjects, and not only those affected by perspective. The lean of a tree trunk, the thrust of a leg, the angle of a car windscreen or the slope of a hill can all be measured effectively in a matter of moments.

061 The Sonic Pencil Spin

Now pay attention at the back—this will require some concentration. There are many pencil spinning techniques and even more variations on them, but here's a relatively easy one, called for some reason that probably defies reason, the 'Sonic'. (See also the 'Thumb-around' 011)

This is a trick that's impossible to mess up. It requires absolutely no practice. There is no way that you'll spend most of the morning flipping the flipping thing half way across the room, making your hand ache, you head spin, and plumbing depths of frustration previously unknown in your sheltered life. No way at all. No Sir. Not on your nelly.

Hold a full-length pencil between index and middle finger with the blunt end lodged behind the fleshy fold of skin in the crook of the thumb. The fingers should be slightly bent inwards.

Extend the fingers outwards, causing the end of the pencil to clear the thumb and snap outwards rapidly. This snapping action creates the necessary momentum. At this point it will flail around unimpressively unless you are prepared for a quick move of the fingers to bring it into your control.

As the pencil snaps out and swings upward, move your index finger back, allowing the pencil to continue its swing around.

Bringing your index finger back in, just a touch, then causes the pencil to complete its graceful arc and return to its original position. And then you can repeat the movements over and over again, flawlessly.

At least that's the theory. All of this happens in fractions of a second. It is not an intellectual pursuit, but an almost unconscious physical activity requiring muscle memory that only comes through many repetitions. If you get disheartened, just remember: schoolchildren can do this, but then they do have quite a lot of time on their hands.

062 Fashion Illustration

I don't get fashion. In fact, I don't like it. Perhaps it's just me, but if I find a nice, comfortable pair of trousers or a cosy jumper I want to return to the shop after a few years and get another one like it. I don't want to be told they haven't stocked that item for many 'seasons'. But there are an awful lot of people who like to keep up with ever fleeting trends and peruse the latest look, so there must be something in it, I reluctantly suppose. But whatever I or anyone else may think about the fashion industry, it has given us some wonderful illustration and design over the years.

If it tickles your fancy to have a go at fashion illustration, you have behind your ear the very tool for the job. What ends up glittering on the catwalks of Milan originally takes shape as pencil jottings on paper. First you'll need a template figure, or 'croquis' to drape with your groovy designs. Don't think for a moment that you can get a friend to pose for you; fashion figures are unlike any real-life person. They are unfeasibly tall and adopt poses beyond the extremes of human articulation. So begin by drawing an elongated skeleton figure with a small head and very long limbs. Get some swing into the figure by sloping the shoulders and hips in opposite directions.

Over your stick framework add the flesh and contours of the figure. Bear in mind that the fashion figure is usually around ten heads tall (a real person may be seven to eight of their head lengths in height). To check that your figure is balanced, strike a vertical line down from the centre of the torso. It should fall between the feet, otherwise your figure will appear to be toppling over, and that wouldn't look very graceful, would it now?

Once you are satisfied with a rough croquis, you can use it over and over for any number of new designs. Place a sheet of layout paper over it and trace through the shape of the figure. Then you are free to go to town and clothe your figure in whatever outlandish vestments you can dream up. Bear in mind the types and weights of fabrics and how they hang off or hug around the figure. Practice of drawing the people around you will develop your feel for how cloth sits around the body (see 026).

TIP: For a harmonious costume design, it's a good idea to repeat some details, motifs or textures.

Designing is usually quite messy, involving lots of changes and rubbings out. But that's okay—it's all part of the creative process. A finished fashion illustration should look clean and spontaneous, so your designs will need re-drafting. A fresh sheet of layout paper goes over the rough design, allowing you to draw it again with confident, crisp lines (see tracing 016). Keep the face and hair simple, and do try to make her pretty; the public is perfectly willing to accept emaciated, elongated mutants but no one wants to see a plain face.

063 Everlasting Chewing Gum

Wailing and gnashing of teeth are facts of life. We may as well accept this and get on with things. Issues like exams, work, love affairs and trying to connect to the Internet can often induce stress and compulsive behaviour which are not very good for you.

So take it out on your pencil. Whilst working your teeth into the wrong end of a pencil you can't be gnawing your fingernails to the quick, stuffing donuts into your face or knocking back the hard stuff. The incense cedar from which pencils are made is selected for its softness and resistance to splintering. So your mouthparts will be safe and once you get it going it releases a taste that is not at all unpleasant. Best of all, the chewing action relieves anxiety and actually helps to focus the mind and bring you closer to a resolution of your plight.

(When you go for a job interview, it might be a good idea to glance around the office pencil pots. The number of chewed pencils could provide a revealing insight into what awaits you.)

I would advise you to select a pencil that is not coated with too much paint and lacquer, although if your problems feel as bad as mine you'll soon work through the most stubborn of coatings. Oh, and make sure there's no gob of earwax lurking in ambush (see 057). We all know how horrible that tastes, right kids?

Draw in Deep Space

Here are two rapid sketches from my pocket sketchbook. They are both passable donkeys but you will notice that one of them appears to be somehow *closer*. The fact is that I was standing much closer to it when drawing so its parts that were closest to my eyes appear exaggeratedly large compared with its more distant hindquarters. Drawn from further away, the difference in relative distance of the other donkey's body parts from my eye was much reduced. This is an effect that can be played around with to create a sense of involvement with a subject or to emphasise spatial distance between elements of a picture.

I utilsed this principle in drawing this digger, intentionally positioning myself sitting down very close to the scoop, making the cabin part appear very much smaller in comparison. In my initial drawing I also exaggerated the size of the scoop to further emphasise the great reach of the machine. Content with the general proportions, I then worked up the details of the cab using a fairly hard pencil (HB).

Moving on to the arm, I switched to a softer pencil (2B) to increase the tonal contrast in this closer element of the picture, employing the effects of aerial perspective (030).

For the scoop, I used a yet softer pencil (6B) and worked the shading very dark whilst keeping the lighter parts pure white paper, for maximum tonal contrast. To finish I added some faint background foliage and generally tweaked the tones of the drawing to create a smooth tonal transition from near distance to far.

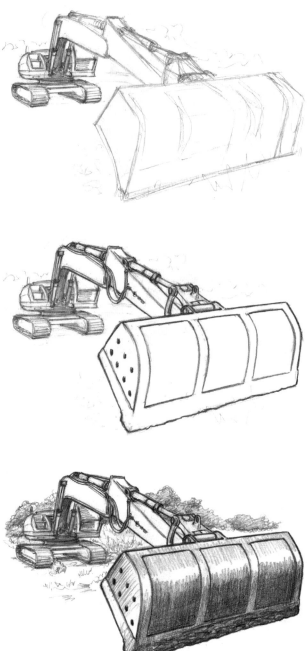

065 Repel Moths

If ever you have dug out a favourite jumper and found holes where there shouldn't be, then you will know the nuisance of clothes moths. If ever you have rummaged through clothing in a jumble sale, then you will know the nasty reek of mothballs. However, thanks to the pencil, there is another way to repel the little blighters.

The secret is in the particular wood of which pencils are made. Incense cedar is subtly aromatic and not at all unpleasant to human nostrils. The moth, however, is not so keen. Now, merely chucking a pencil into your wardrobe is not going to do any good at all; you need more surface area of the wood to release the fragrance. So you use shavings. Instead of emp-

tying your pencil sharpener into the bin or compost heap, decant the contents into little bags of gauze or loosely woven fabric and hang them amongst your clothing. That should get the moths fluttering suicidally towards the nearest light bulb. Every few weeks give the bags a little shake to release the odour and regularly refresh them with new shavings.

066 Smudge Drawing

You've probably noticed that the softer the pencils you use, the more prone they are to smudging. And when your hand has accidentally smeared across a fine bit of drawing, you've probably muttered words you wouldn't want your mum to hear. This is, unfortunately, something of an occupational hazard, though it can be avoided by placing a clean piece of paper under your drawing hand whilst you work. Or you could embrace smudging and make it a feature of your work.

Smudged pencil marks look dirty, and that can be a good thing if you want a subject to look dirty. As I sketched this fine vehicle with a soft pencil, I used my fingertips to smudge my rough shading on the bodywork. As well as an appropriately scruffy feel, it also smoothed the transitions of tone, which helped to describe the curved surfaces. I was careful to keep my hand well clear of the darker outlining though—it would not do to smudge the whole drawing.

Smudged pencil marks lose their crisp edges, and that can be a good thing if you are wont to draw something with soft edges. This dear little baby owl was little more than a ball of fluff, so I smudged some roughly shaded marks to form his body shape. I then used the point of the same soft pencil to add a few details here and there to give him some character and to contrast with the soft texture.

TIP: Protect finished drawings from unwanted smudging by spraying lightly with artist's fixative spray, available from art shops, or with hairspray, available from chemists at a fraction of the price.

 # Support a Young Plant

Much like children, gangly young plants such as runner beans or tomatoes may need a little gentle support until they are mature enough to fend for themselves. If a plantling succumbs to a touch of sagginess, push a pencil, directly upright, an inch or so into the soil beside it to form a kind of splint. Tie plant and pencil together somewhere near the top with a loose loop of string or similar. Thus the pencil will help to keep the plant upright until it is big and strong enough to be planted outside and make its way in the world. If only children required so little support to reach maturity.

Pencil Shavings Pictures

When using a pencil sharpener, focused as we are on the task at hand, it's not surprising that we overlook the delicate shavings that curl out. It seems a shame to discard all these pretty scalloped scrolls—perhaps they could inspire further outpourings of creative genius . . . or at least some quirky little cartoons.

With a little care, it's quite easy to make some really long coils of raw material that can be broken to any desired length. There are two basic approaches: stick then draw or draw then stick. For the former, take a section of shaving, glue it flat on some blank paper and then complete a picture with a few lines of drawing.

TIP: If you use a glue stick, apply it to the paper rather than the shavings, otherwise you may break them apart.

It's probably easier to do a drawing first and then stick the shavings in just the right places. That way you can do something more ambitious, such as a dragon, landscape or exotic costume and decorate it with many overlapping layers of shavings. Alternatively, you need not actually stick anything down at all. Children will be entertained if you present them with a blank face or figure and a pile of shavings they can move around to form wacky hair, costumes and accessories. Perhaps they can then stick down their best designs and add more drawing to complete a character.

(069) Grid Games

Snake

Some years ago I gave in to the unstoppable tide of technology and bought a portable telephone. (I believe they are generally called 'mobiles' but I've yet to see one that moves autonomously.) On my shiny new 'mobile' were some games and I wasted an hour or two playing one called Snake. I soon tired of competing against a lump of plastic, however. It is so much more rewarding to play against a real live, flesh and blood, gloat-worthy human being. A variant of the Snake game can be played with a pleasingly low-tech pencil and paper and a competitive adversary.

Draw a matrix of dots. Here I've done a 5 x 5 square, but it can be of any shape or size you fancy. Each player starts at a point one dot in from opposite corners. They take turns to draw segments of their snake by marking a horizontal or vertical line from the previous dot to an adjacent dot. A snake must not touch either itself or the opponent's snake. The first player unable to move is a loser. In this demonstration, the snake on the right has nowhere left to go and really should try harder next time.

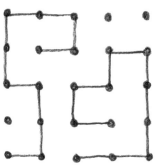

Domineering

Here's another game for two players, also known as Cross cram or Stop-Gate, which starts on a similar grid of any size. Player one is horizontal, player two is vertical and they take turns to link pairs of adjacent dots. No dot can be linked more than once. The first player unable to make a fresh link faces the infinite shame of defeat. It's as simple as that. Here the game is lost by the vertical player who has no free pair of dots left to link.

Dots and Boxes

This game is known by many names, but whether you call it Dots and Boxes, Dots, Boxes, Dot Boxing, Smart Dots, Dots and Dashes, Squares, Square-It, Paddocks, Pigs in a Pen, or the Reverend Rodney 'Susan' Smith, it's the same game. And what a jolly good game it is—more complex and brain teasing than at first it seems.

Generally, this is played on a smaller matrix than Snakes or Domineering, usually limited to 3x3, 4x4, or 5x5, but in theory there is no limit to its size. Two players take turns to join adjacent dots either horizontally or vertically. A player who completes the fourth side of a box claims it with her mark or initial and then they must draw another line. (It may sound like a bonus to get a 'free' go, but it can be your undoing.) When the grid is fully filled in, the player with more boxes initialled claims victory and has every right to perform celebratory naked star jumps in every room of the house.

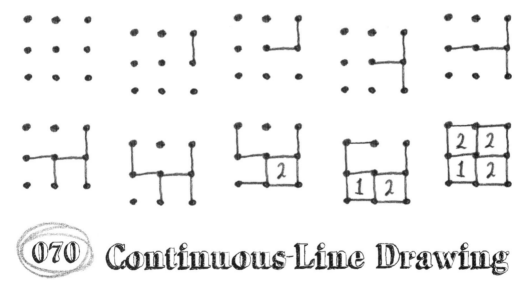

(070) Continuous-Line Drawing

Many amateur draughtsmen suffer from debilitating perfectionism—a tendency to labour too much over drawings and fret over getting them 'wrong'. Well, here is a good technique to help you loosen up and set your drawing hand free.

The basic principle is to keep your pencil in contact with the paper throughout the drawing. Start in one corner and work your way around the subject, jumping from one part to another almost as if tracing an outline. Keep your eye moving between subject and drawing. Don't worry if the line comes to a dead end or runs off the page—just carry on from another point. The dimensions will naturally drift and the drawing may take on a distorted look, but work with it until you have made all the ends join up and filled in the whole outline.

You may initially think your continuous line drawing looks like the left-handed tracings of a Neanderthal. But don't be put off. Make several attempts and then set them to one side. When you review them later, you'll probably find something really quite quirky and interesting that you would never have drawn by conventional methods. Maybe you'll even be inspired to let go of some prejudices and embrace a looser, more liberated style.

You may like to try working over a very basic framework of guidelines. Maybe you can continue developing a drawing beyond the continuous line, reinforcing prominent lines, adding tone and texture, light and shade. Like all techniques, it can be only the starting point of a whole field of exploration and development.

The Pencil-Up-Nose Illusion

The following trick must be approached with caution if you do not want to pierce your brain. You will need a featureless pencil: one without lettering or lateral markings, although vertical stripes are acceptable. Face your audience confidently and invite them to inspect your prop and satisfy themselves that it is indeed a real, solid, wooden pencil. Insert the BLUNT END into a nostril. (The pointy end of a pencil should NEVER be allowed to enter any orifice.) With the back of your hand facing the audience and keeping a very loose grip, slowly move your hand up the length of the pencil. You may do this in a slick, smooth motion, or grimace and struggle as if forcing the object against nature, depending on your performance style. With the pencil hidden behind your hand and wrist, it will appear to be inserted up your nose.

The tricky bit is to create the impression of pulling it out again. You have to move your hand back down the pencil's shaft without the blunt end being allowed to leave the nose. The average nostril should afford just enough grip, although it may also be helpful to breathe in steadily through the nose during this procedure. If at any time the audience can see either end of the pencil, the illusion will be instantly shattered. Once your fingers have again found the pointy end, the pencil may be withdrawn and you can bask in the warmth of tumultuous applause (and use your magician's hanky to wipe off any bits of bogey).

N.B. This trick should never be performed to impressionable youngsters or any adult who may be too dim to realize it's a trick.

 # Caricature by Head Shape

A useful trick for getting a caricature off to a good start is to lead with the shape of the head. Identify something particular about your target: a large forehead, prominent jaw, elongated face or such like. Here I am working on chubby songster, Elton John. To me, it's the broad mouth and fat cheeks that are the prime features to develop. His rounded upper head and trademark hair 'style' can be reduced in size to give scale to the lower face.

The features can now be copied straight onto the new exaggerated head shape, which will guide their placement and scale. Here I started with the mouth, which then suggested how large the chin should be. I sacrificed the size of the nose for the sake of the mouth size. All the features are all drawn in very loosely at this stage.

TIP: For a successful caricature, gather several photos of your subject, taken from different angles at different stages of their career. They will give you a better feel for the face and provide a range of accessories to decorate your caricature.

With a basic drawing established, I went on to develop the features, looking carefully at my source photographs and making lots of changes here and there along the way, with copious use of the eraser.

Although most heads are essentially very similar in shape, there is usually something about any individual that can be drawn out into a radically exaggerated head shape. Here, for example, are Shakespeare's swollen cranium and Amy Winehouse's llong equine head and face.

(073) Tests for Breasts

We can all tell the difference between spring and summer, wet and dry, sickness and health. But in the transition from one state to another distinctions are less clear. When precisely does day pass into twilight and can you clearly discern the moment of the twilight's yielding to the curtain of night? Now, I'm guessing here, but I would imagine there's a time in a young lady's passage through life when she needs to judge how well she's developing. When should she start wearing a bra?

There is a simple test she can undertake in the seclusion of her private chamber using nothing more than a pencil. She must push the horizontal pencil up against the underside of a breast and then let go. If the pencil drops to the floor, she can probably save her pocket money for now. But if the weight of the breast holds the pencil in place, then the time has come for her to seek the advice of a reputable lingerie merchant.

Apparently, you can get different sorts of bras that offer varying levels of support. Some of them are adjustable, so that you can get them just right for your own level of endowment. One aim, I am informed, is to acquire an especially well formed cleavage. But how can you tell what constitutes the perfect cleavage? Once all the clasps and guy ropes are in place, test by placing a pencil vertically between the breasts, if it falls to the floor, conventional thinking reckons you need to ratchet your bra up another notch or two. If your cleavage can keep a whole pencil case aloft, you can probably relax the tension a touch.

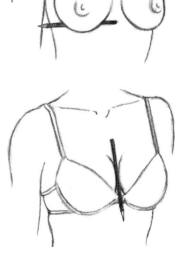

TIP: These tests are of no equivalent use to a teenage boy.

(074) Draw a Still Life

Still life is a slightly confusing term. It refers to a small-scale arrangement of inanimate objects, usually on a tabletop. Still life subjects definitely don't move; no problem there. But on the other hand, they're not exactly alive, which I suppose is why they remain still. Anyway there we are, they're called what they're called, and who are we to argue with centuries of tradition?

Drawing a still life has much to commend it. You're completely in control of what objects you draw, what you leave out, how it's all arranged and how it's lit. You can do it sitting down, in a nice warm room, with a glass of wine and your favourite Barry Manilow CD in the background. And you can take your time because, as I believe I may have mentioned, nothing is going to move or lose patience with you—until the family wants to eat at the table, that is.

First, select your subject. You could choose objects for variety of shape, size, texture or, conversely, for their similarities. Maybe a theme would turn you on—items relating to a craft or gardening, old toys, holiday souvenirs, natural forms or geometric shapes and so on. In olden days the 'memento mori' was a popular theme—grizzly objects relating to death and decay to remind us of our inescapable moribund destiny. Nice.

Plonk your chosen objects on the table and see how they look. Unless you're very lucky, they'll need a lot of jiggling around to make a pleasing arrangement. It usually works well to keep the arrangement compact, with objects butting up against each other, some in front of and on top of each other and maybe a single stand-alone item. If you're working with light from the window, or from a ceiling light, you may have to move the table around to get the light hitting at a suitable angle. A movable light source is much more convenient. You will probably find it useful to make some thumbnail sketches (see 046). Now there should be nothing between you, your pencil and an hour or two of restful sketching.

Some of the best still-life subjects are out there waiting for you to notice them. Maybe you'll come across a collection of pots in a garden, a pile of shoes in the hallway, some cushions and newspapers strewn in the corner of a sofa or some tools left out on a workbench. Such arrangements make for especially pleasing subjects, seeming real and somehow reflective of life . . . Oh, I get it now.

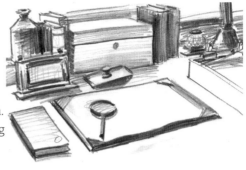

TIP: Make yourself a viewfinder by cutting a rectangular hole in a piece of cardboard. This will act as a kind of frame to look at a potential subject through, helping you to select the parts you want to draw and to visualise how they will be arranged on the page.

(075) Makeshift Dice

Once a group of people have reached the often painful accord to play a board game, it can take much more heated debate to decide which game to play. By which time it will cause the greatest frustration if the dice are missing from the box. But fear not—simply reach for a hexagonal pencil and a sharp knife.

Just like a die, a hexagonal pencil has six evenly weighted sides. Cut a series of notches into the sides of the pencil to label them one to six. Make sure that the numbers of notches on opposite sides of the pencil add up to seven. So one notch goes opposite six, two opposite five, and three opposite four. Your cylindrical die may now be rolled across the table and when it comes to rest, the number of notches on the uppermost side can be easily read. For games that require two dice, either use two pencils or roll twice.

(076) Coin Rubbings

We may think of ourselves as grown up and beyond childish things, but perhaps we are denying ourselves simple pleasures unnecessarily. Have you done a jigsaw puzzle lately? They're really quite fun, once in a while. Is there any good reason why you should not dabble with Lego, or play conkers, or run a stick along some railings? I'd draw the line at eating bogies, but maybe that's just me.

You will find there remains something just a little bit magical about making coin rubbings. If you've never done it, you're in for a treat. First you'll need to fish out a coin from down the back of the sofa. Place it on a flat surface and lay some fairly thin paper on top. Holding both items still, rub the side of a pencil over the surface and a remarkably detailed impression of the coin will emerge. Experiment with different or multiple directions of shading. Carefully erase scrappy marks around the edges, or cut your coins out with scissors and stick on black paper. The challenge is to make them as flawlessly neat as you can.

TIP: Fix your coins onto the table top with sticky gum or rolled up sticky tape to keep them from shifting around. Any tiny movement between coin and paper will replicate the disconcerting and all-too-familiar effect of staring at loose change whilst drunk.

Encourage your children to join in the fun. Kids love crafty things. They also like collecting things, and coin rubbings are a good way for them to build up a coin collection without the temptation of legal tender hanging around.

077 Exercise your Eyes

No one can argue that we're all growing older. While this is great news if you're a child, once you get past 25 you stop growing and start decaying. Within another ten years or so you'll probably find that your arms are not as long as they used to be as you struggle to focus on the book in your outstretched hand. Maybe you should get glasses? Or maybe you should get your pencil out…

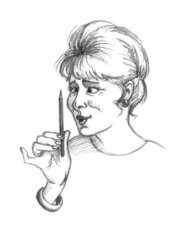

Here's a simple exercise recommended by opticians to strengthen the muscles of the eye that enable us to focus. Hold the pencil at arms length and focus on its tip. Gradually bring the pencil closer to your eyes, holding your focus all the while. Keep going until it nearly touches your nose. It will feel like quite a strain at first, that's because it is working seldom-exercised muscles. Repeat the process several times over and do it every day. You should soon notice some improvement in your focusing and hold back the day when you have to give in to the inevitable.

This exercise is also good practice for going cross-eyed, which is always a sure-fire way to amuse children and help them pass the time while they are waiting to grow older.

078 Frottage

Looking up the origins of this term, it appears to have two meanings—and it's probably best to gloss over the second one. As far as we are concerned here, frottage refers to the act of rubbing a pencil over a textured surface, much like coin rubbings (see 076), except that frottage is more random in nature. The technique was developed in the 1920s by Max Ernst, whose surreal imagination saw strange images in the grain of his wooden floor.

Any texture will do so long as it is fairly robust. Natural textures such as stone, brick, leaves, sea-shells and bark work well. Synthetic materials like meshes and industrial surfaces can also make for effective textures, though less random and therefore less likely to inspire your visionary genius.

The technique is simple: place a sheet of paper over your chosen surface and rub over it with the side of a soft pencil. A typical approach is to look for images emerging from the random marks and then draw into them and erase areas to develop your visions. The example here started as a rubbing of the slate tiles on my bathroom floor. Initially it suggested mountainous scenery so I left a clear area for the sky. But turning it round, it looked like a brooding stormy sky, so I changed my mind and filled in the ground by rubbing over a section of fence panel in my garden. I think it looks like an atmospheric ancient hillside, but my wife immediately saw an aerial view of the sea lapping onto a sandy shore. And who is to say which of us is right? (Except that she's always right.)

Textural rubbings can also be used with a predetermined aim. To save some laborious mark making for the rough surface of this Indian rhino, I used a cheese grater, moving the paper around to avoid too regular a pattern. For the ribs I used a section of fence panel again.

079 Retrieve Problem Toast

It is a well-known fact that most serious accidents occur in the home. And one of the most common, and potentially lethal, areas of danger centres on the seemingly harmless toaster. When a crumpet, bun or slice of artisan bread does not pop up above the top of the toaster it may seem appropriate to poke your fingers in to retrieve it. But you may very well get a nasty burn. Aware of this danger, people often fish around inside with a knife, but that is even more dangerous, tempting a genuinely dramatic electrical explosion. And then you would be toast.

A wooden pencil, however, does not conduct heat or electricity, so it is much the safer option for fishing out your toasted goodies. This, however, is as far as the pencil's usefulness goes in this area; thorough tests undertaken for this book have proven quite conclusively that pencils are all but useless for slicing bread or spreading jam.

TIP: Let's not take any chances; always disconnect any appliance from the mains before poking around inside.

080 Lines of Action

Take a look at the curved line in the corner of this page. It may look quite insignificant, you may not even have noticed it, but you'd be surprised how effective such a line can be in figure drawing. It is an example of a 'line of action', a guideline used by all sorts of artists to capture the essence of a pose or gesture and to endow the drawn figure with dynamism, grace and movement.

These two sketches, one from a life drawing class the other done in an art museum, are both based around similar lines of action. Sketching in the line of thrust that runs through a body gives immediate direction to a pose or posture, greatly aiding and influencing the drawing. Lines of action can be observed in all sorts of poses, even sleeping and sitting subjects. Identifying them will get your figure drawings off to a flying start (see 088).

Action lines are also useful for drawing figures from the imagination. Comic book artists and fashion illustrators make particular use of them to guide the action of their characters and models. These two sketches again make use of the same line of action.

In the cartoon world where gestures can be exaggerated wildly, action lines really come into their own. Here our action line gives this poor fellow a backward thrust that emphasises the weight of his load. Exaggerating the same curve gives the lady a seductive wiggle of the hips.

Of course, action lines can be as varied as the figures drawn around them. A stately old gent requires only a gentle tilt forward to get him strolling along, but a sprightly wee lass runs at full pelt with an action line that leans so far forward it's almost horizontal.

Comic and cartoon artists always aim to depict a powerful gesture at an extreme point of the action, either coiling back in preparation or following through at the other end. Again the action line guides the drawing and unifies the figure in its intention, passing through the whole body, the arms and, in this case, the weapon too.

(081) Hangman

Most readers will be familiar with the age-old game of hangman. If you're not, you're in for a treat. I'll quickly run through the basic order of play before getting on to some tips for sure-fire dominance.

This is a game for two players: one the 'executioner' and one the 'defendant'. The executioner holds the pencil and thinks of a fiendishly tricky word, marking on some scrap paper a dash for each letter of their word. The defendant takes guesses at letters that may feature in the word. Correct guesses are written in their correct places above the dashes. Incorrect guesses are marked down underneath a rudimentary drawing, which grows with a new pencil stroke for every wrong guess. The drawing builds up to a complete gallows and swinging corpse. Once the last limb is in place the defendant is dead, but if he can correctly guess the word before the drawing is complete he can escape this grizzly fate and assume superiority. However, incorrect guesses at the complete word also count toward his downfall.

There is some dispute over how many lines make up the gallows, and this needs to be established before playing lest an overzealous executioner hasten the defendant's demise by constructing rickety gallows without a floor plane and adequate bracing. The illustration here represents a generally accepted form of gallows, completed in eleven strokes of the pencil.

An inexperienced executioner will usually yield to the temptation to choose long and impressive words, but this only increases the defendant's chance of striking a hit with each guess. It is much more devious to choose short words, made up of uncommonly used letters. DRY, FUG or ZIT are good candidates.

Avoiding vowels often works well, as in RHYTHM, HYMN or LYMPH. Or you could make those vowels work in your favour by choosing words that feature them in unusual pairings (like BAZAAR, VACUUM or SKIING). Words with unusual combinations of letters (like PHLEGM, TWELFTH or SPHINX) are also good choices.

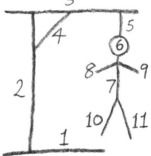

TIP: Unless you want to sour relations, never choose words found only in the pages of a Tolkien novel.

As a defendant, you can save yourself some early heartache by ignoring the vowels. Once you have some consonants in place you can often guess at which vowels logically belong in between. Never guess at the whole word. If you have a hunch, guess the remaining letters individually; if your guess is wrong, you will still have succeeded in eliminating possible letters.

 082 Juxtaposition

It may sound like a la-di-dah, swallowed-a-dictionary, arty-farty word, but 'juxtaposition' really only means putting things together—a simple meaning but a powerful artistic device. Combining things that are not usually seen together in the same space opens up all sorts of possibilities for how a drawing can be read and invites interpretation of meaning.

It does not take advanced drawing skill to combine disparate subjects for humorous, attention-grabbing or satirical effect. It really is as simple as drawing one thing and then drawing something else to go with it. It often helps if you adhere to a fairly consistent drawing language throughout: similar weight of mark, similar lighting and so on. It also helps if the different elements interact in some way. They may touch, overlap, adjoin and fix attention on each other or any other device that presents them in a single reality.

In this simple example, an element of story telling is introduced. The cat had already got up and wandered off by the time I decided to draw a toy mouse in front of it. I then adjusted the cat's gaze to connect the objects and added the cat's extended claws.

I sketched this light-hearted assemblage in a museum, combining elements of a mounted stag's head with a stuffed rabbit. It looks quite believable, until you contemplate such a rabbit trying to scuttle into its burrow.

Can a fish ride a bicycle? Would an apple fill your living room? Does a wasp have the head of a tiger? At the point of a pencil all this, and more, is possible. In the 1920s and 30s talented nutters like Salvador Dali and Rene Magritte based much of their Surrealist art around dream-like juxtapositions and distortions of reality. The more random the combinations, the more surreal and intriguing the picture.

These two items do not interact in any way except in their presentation in the same space. They were drawn at different times in different sketchbooks. By placing them together the viewer is invited to draw parallels and consider a meaning in their juxtaposition—helped by the 'mirroring' of both objects' forms and scale.

 **Chopsticks**

Clever people the Chinese. They invented paper, matches, gunpowder, pasta, umbrellas, playing cards, ice cream, printing, wheelbarrows, great walls and loads of other useful things, including china. With all that lot to busy themselves with, I suppose it's forgivable that they neglected to invent forks. Neither did they invent pencils. But in a strange way they invented things a bit like pencils that act a bit like forks. Chopsticks can be really fiddly. Give me a fork any day, or a spoon, or a nose bag.

Then again, out on your rambles it is not inconceivable (it has happened to me) that you may avail upon the opportunity to eat a portion of whelks or a tasty salad (if that's not a contradiction in terms), but have no utensil with which to transport the foodstuff to your eager mouth. This is when you delve into your adventurer's bag, pull out two cleanish pencils and give thanks to the ancient Chinese.

Chopsticks, needless to say, are in two parts and they perform different functions. First you'll need your anchor, which will remain immobile in your hand. Take one pencil, blunt end facing away from you and hold it in your right (or left, if you're that way inclined) hand, nestled into the crook of your thumb and held firmly against the ring finger. This will work as your anchor and will not move in your hand.

TIP: If your pencils are of different lengths, use the longer one as your anchor.

Grip the second pencil between the tip of the thumb and the first and second fingers. Tap the two business ends on a flat surface to get them even. Now you should be able to move the top pencil up and down against the lower pencil, effectively opening and closing your makeshift chopsticks.

You are now ready to tuck in. Attack your lunch from a 45-degree angle and don't be too ambitious at first. Get used to picking up small solid pieces and work up to big old mouthfuls. Bon appétit!

TIP: Keep your bowl directly under your mouth as you feed. You may find occasional chunks of food dropping from your chopsticks you wouldn't want them rolling down the front of your cardigan.

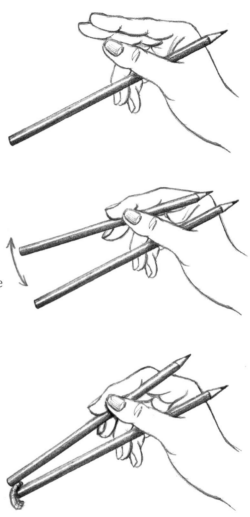

(084) Flick Book Animation

You probably don't realise it, but you are holding in your hand, right now, the empty stage for a lively performance. No, in the other hand; I'm talking about this book, you fool. You see those margins running down the edges of the pages? They are just waiting for you to populate them with a cast of moving pictures.

You have probably seen animation flick books before. If not, I envy you the treat you are about to create for yourself. Here's how:

Start at the back of the book with the right-hand margin of the right-hand page. Do a bold little drawing and make it super simple (if it's too complicated you may soon regret it). Then, turn to the second-from-last page. You should be able to see a faint impression of your original motif through the paper. Now trace it through, but make a tiny, almost insignificant change. On the next page back, draw it again with the change taken another tiny step further. Keep doing this until you either run out of book or the will to live—whichever comes soonest. I'll give you a few minutes.

Finished? OK, a little longer . . .

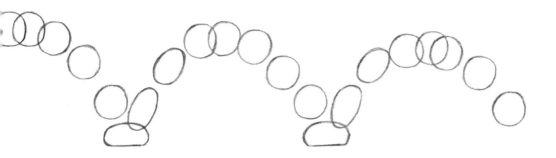

Have you finished now? All right, let's go with what we've got so far. Take the pages of the book in your left hand and flick through the pages at a steady pace. Did you see that? Your drawings moved. That, my friend, is what we call animation. You have created life, or at least the illusion of it. But then, perhaps all of life is nought but an illusion . . .

Anyway, there are many devices that can be explored without rigorous drawing required: A simple dot can be made to move up or along the bottom of the page. It can grow in size, multiply, bounce like a ball or turn into a flower. A line can grow in length, wiggle, sway or curl into a spiral. A small animal can jump, run on the spot or walk right off the page. Hoards of flying monkeys can descend upon a mountain village and reduce it to smoking rubble. When you have filled up all the available space in this book, don't worry; I'm sure you can find plenty of other books around the house, all with lovely empty margins waiting to be brought to life.

085 Pencil Moustache

Admittedly, this is not the most sophisticated use that a pencil has ever been put to. Place the centre of your pencil horizontally under your nose and purse your lips, as if poised for a sloppy kiss. The pencil will remain suspended, like a really unconvincing moustache. If you fear your intention is slightly ambiguous, this can be cleared up in an instant by saying, 'Look at my lovely moustache'. Don't expect riotous mirth or elevation to 'favourite uncle/auntie' status, but you may just succeed in distracting little Johnnie's attention from his computer/feeding trough/cycle of destruction, at least for the few seconds you need to convey a necessary instruction. This is one of the few tips that works better with a short pencil. It does not work so well if you are blessed with a real moustache.

086 Nocturnes and Atmosphere

The broad range of tonal marks you can get from pencils makes them ideally suited to subjects of enigmatic half-light and brooding atmosphere. Whereas a landscape in daylight can be problematic in pencil (see 058), depicting a sombre or sinister scene requires little lightness of touch. Such scenes also allow you to get away with a minimum of detailed drawing. All of which is great news for ham-fisted fudgers like me.

The key to dark and sombre picture making is in the composition. It's often useful to preface a drawing with thumbnails (see 046), drawing with the side of your pencil to set down the blocks of shade that make up the scene in order to identify a framing of tonal balance. Once you have arrived at a pleasing composition, you can really get stuck in.

There's no need for hesitancy here; any
rough under-drawing will soon be lost among
layers of tone. When drawing these twilit
backwaters, I went straight in with the edge
of a soft pencil and scribbled in the main blocks
of grey without concern for texture or precision.

Working from the far distance forward, I
started to add the deeper tones that would bring
form to the landscape, changing my pencil grip
and pressing harder, as necessary. As I worked
down the drawing, towards the foreground, I
introduced some textural marks to describe the
rough scrub and uneven ground surface.

Only in the final stages did I pay any attention to detail. First, though, I used an eraser to
clean off any rough marks on the sky and water
surface. Then I added a few odd details—some
rotten posts, reflections and so on— to give
character to the location. I tweaked the tones
and horizon silhouettes and then left it alone,
mainly because I didn't want it to get too heavy
and sombre but also because there was a very
fine pub just a short distance away.

(087) The Disappearing Pencil

Anyone with a pencil and a modicum of guile can perfect this illusion in just a few minutes. The effect is to make the pencil magically disappear and then reappear. It is performed in mere seconds, but the effect on the audience should last some while longer. The secret is in blatant misdirection.

Stand with your left side to the audience and tell them that you intend to push a pencil straight through your hand. Hold the pencil in your right hand, in a writing grip and extend your left hand in front of you, palm uppermost. The audience, thirsty for blood, will naturally fix its attention on the left hand.

Bending your arm at the elbow, lift your right hand and pencil up as far as your ear, and then swing it down swiftly to make contact with the left hand, as you emit the word, 'One!' In a rhythmic sequence, repeat this action for the count of 'Two!' At the third time of raising the pencil, deposit it behind your right ear before you bring the hand down on 'Three!' and press your fingers into your left palm. Rather than the painful display they had been looking forward to, the audience will note that the pencil has instead evaporated. You may pretend to share their surprise and examine your empty hands, but keep your right side turned away throughout.

To make the pencil reappear, perform the sequence again with your empty hand, this time retrieving the pencil from your ear after the second stroke.

TIP: This trick is most effective when performed for a just one or two people who are standing close beside you. The arc through which the arm swings will be too wide for their field of vision.

(088) Life Drawing

I can think of worse ways to spend time than sitting in a warm
room studying the contours of a naked young body. Sitcoms
would have it that the life drawing class is a scene ripe for winks,
nudges and saucy jokes, or perhaps there is the inherent suggestion of something lascivious about it. In reality, though, there is
no titillation and no intimate exchange between subject and artist.
The atmosphere is very matter-of-fact, and being quite expensive,
everyone is keen to get on and do some work. And it's not all gorgeous young lovelies. In fact, it turns out that the most interesting
models are those with a few miles on the clock. Still, I can think of
worse ways to spend time.

The most striking thing about life drawing, other than the nudist
in the corner, is how quickly the time goes. It's easy to slip into a
comfortable reverie polishing your minor masterpiece while three
hours whizz quietly by. You'll get much more bang for your buck
if you determine to make the time count. Do lots
of drawings. Vary the time you allow yourself from
just a minute or so to maybe twenty minutes at the
most. Draw small pictures. Draw BIG pictures. Vary
your viewpoints, crouch on the floor. stand on a chair,
move around the room and encourage the model to
change poses regularly.

Now, how to draw the human figure...

Identify the essence of the pose. Most poses
will have a clear action line running through them
(see 080), but even a body at rest will centre around
definite curves. Mark the main thrust and then quickly
sketch the basic masses of head and trunk. The limbs
can be mere lines at first. Then add details onto and

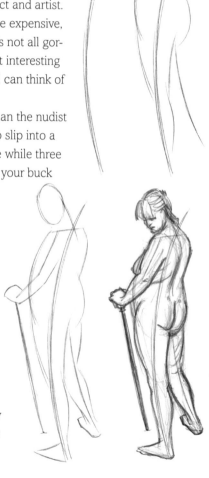

103

around your initial framework. You may like to make some rough measurements (see 052 sight sizing) but don't spend too long establishing the basic figure. Bear it in mind that arms, legs and necks can be a lot longer than you might think.

Keep everything very loose and free and gradually tighten up to the level that you require. Treat the hair as a mass, an abstract shape and don't bother about shading it in; it isn't important. The face too can be treated as a few basic features. The object here is not portraiture. Try to get some form and character into the hands and feet, which are all too often ignored. They're not hard if you initially draw them as masses and then break them down into separate parts without getting too fiddly. Knees, elbows and ankles are hard and bony so use sharper marks here. Reserve softer marks for fleshier parts like buttocks, bellies and breasts.

The life class is not the place to aim for beautifully finished drawings, although beauty can come out of the simplest drawings. Aim instead at increasing your knowledge and experience of drawing the human body. The more sketches you produce, the more chances you have of all the parts coming together in a satisfying drawing or two.

 Consequences

Here's a silly game all the family can play. In fact it works best when you have a range of ages and life experiences to draw upon. There are several different versions to chose from, all following the same principle. Each player starts with a pencil and a strip of scrap paper (a piece of A4 torn in half lengthways would be about right.) Players take turns to write or draw on the paper, working from the top down. After their turn, the players fold over the paper to hide their work before passing it on to the next player who then continues without knowing what has gone before. When all stages are complete, the pieces of paper are unfolded and the contents revealed to all.

Story Consequences

In this version, players contribute elements of a story, which will emerge over eight prescribed steps. The steps are:

> 1) (boy's name)
> 2) met... (girl's name)
> 3) in / at...

4) He said...

5) She said...

6) He did...

7) She did...

8) As a consequence...

The results can be bizarre, amusing and sometimes quite revealing. Perhaps they may go something like this:

'Nelson Mandela met Mum at the end of the road. He said "I want to ride my bike". She said "The cushions are lumpy". He threw up. She took her shoes off. As a consequence they held hands and strode off into the sunset'.

Poetry Consequences

If the company demands a little more sophistication, try this version. The first player writes a line of bad poetry, taking care to follow a simple rhythm and end on an easy rhyme. Here the first line remains visible to the next player and only when they have responded with the next line in the poem does the first line get folded back. Each successive player folds back the line before theirs before handing the paper on. For this game, stick to four lines, or if you want to go to eight lines, agree to start a new rhyme for the fifth turn. Here's an example:

Of all the ways a man can fell a tree,
The best of all, I'm sure you would agree,
Is having someone softly stroke your knee,
The way you should behave in company?
A gentleman will always doff his hat,
To any passing dog or bird or cat,
An elephant would seem quite big and fat,
And if he fell upon you, you'd go splat!

Picture Consequences

Perhaps the best-known and most generally amusing version of this game is done with drawing. The first player draws a head and folds the paper back so that just the lines of the neck are showing. Following players add further body parts, always allowing a tiny amount of their drawing to peep out for the next player to join on to. A complete figure will emerge, perhaps in as few as three steps (head/body/legs) or you can break it down further (upper head/lower head/torso/hips/legs/feet), depending on the number of players. The resulting mutants will delight all the contributors.

It really doesn't matter if anyone's individual efforts are unimpressive—that's part of the fun. The principle here is to get children and adults involved on an equal footing. Mind you, if you think playing this game will teach children valuable lessons about the consequences of their actions, you obviously haven't met many children.

090 Loose Perspective

Although it can be useful to understand the principles of perspective they don't always need to be rigorously observed. Cunning selection of scenes and subjects will require of you only a general awareness of perspective and need little or no perspective guidelines or vanishing points.

From a distance, the effects of perspective are much reduced and it becomes a minimal feature of a drawing. I sketched this group of buildings from the opposite side of a lake, far enough away that the angles of receding lines were barely discernable, leaving me free to concentrate on the more interesting diagonals of the roofs.

Very old, wooden-framed buildings gradually settle and warp over the centuries, resulting in skewed and undulating lines and few right angles. Thus, there is no benefit to drafting anything but a very loose and general perspective grid, if you need one at all. All angles (including verticals) may be judged roughly by eye and any errors will only add to the subject's 'olde worlde' charm.

091 Empty Your Tubes

Imagine you're making a Bolognaise sauce. You reach for the tomato puree to find that the tube is almost empty. The shop is fifteen minutes walk away and your guests are due in ten. Surely even the best quality 4B pencil cannot get you out of such a scrape.

But try this: take fore-mentioned pencil and lay it across the crimped bottom end of the tube. Press down on a firm surface as you roll the tube around the pencil. By the time it reaches the top, you should have a good length of paste straining to be unleashed into the pan: a meal's worth of product that would otherwise have gone into the bin. And when finished, slide the pencil out, return it to your hankie pocket or behind your ear and discard the now properly empty tube.

Toothpaste, creams and ointments, glue, paint and any similarly packaged products can be liberated in the same way. And, by the way, if you still don't have enough puree, use ketchup. It's pretty much the same stuff.

092 Challenge Conventional Views

Considering how very much visual material is generated by the modern world it's surprising how conventional most of it is and how restricted it is in scope. Look for pictures of cars on the Internet; you can find literally millions and nearly all of them are from a front, three-quarter, eye-level view. Women may spend hours agonising over their hairstyles, yet almost never do we see a picture of the back of their beautifully coiffed locks.

If you have the desire to use your pencil for creative purposes you will have the option at every turn to look at things in fresh ways. You are free to move around a subject and choose your own angle of view. That is not to say that you need to seek out the wackiest aspects of every subject—the back end of a cat is rarely going to inspire a more satisfying drawing than its front end—but you would do well to least consider your options.

For drawing portraits, the most obvious, common and boring view is directly from the front. Fine for a passport photo, but rarely exciting. But for certain other subjects this same angle of view is one that goes largely unexploited, so it can be surprisingly arresting. A zoo aquarium gave me the opportunity to observe and sketch a piranha from this untypically formal viewpoint.

Another front view, but here the pig is all but obscured. It would have been quite easy to look over the gate and draw a complete pig. However, getting down to the pig's eye level and showing only a narrow strip of the creature creates a drawing of more character.

Getting above or below a subject can provide you with new takes on the familiar. People tend to think they know their surroundings pretty well. It is the job of the artist to see things differently and to offer fresh perspectives that make the viewer re-appraise truths they had previously never thought to challenge—quite a lofty ambition for the humble pencil.

(093) Doodle Drawings

It is rarely fully comprehended how unique drawings are. Every time you set down a few marks on paper you have effectively made a drawing that has never been drawn precisely the same before, not in the whole, multi-millennial history of man's creativity. This randomness can be harnessed to create wacky characters, creatures or monsters that one could never dream up consciously.

Take a scrap of paper, close your eyes and make a swift and random scrawl. Then gaze into the shape you have made to find the beast that lurks within. As humans we are biologically programmed to react to the very slightest suggestion of a face.

When you have worked out what the drawing could be, add some more marks to give life to your creation. Here I have used different parts of the same scribble to make two different grotesque faces.

Turn it through 90 degrees and another different character emerges, and turned again, yet another may be found.

The same technique can be employed to create fanciful devices, alien plants or whole fantasy landscapes. The only limit is your imagination.

(094) Move Mountains

It may sound facile to say that a pencil is not a camera. Of course not, neither is it a fire engine or a plate of lentils. But it is particularly liberating to acknowledge that when we draw we are not limited to photographic reality. Artists through the ages have played fast and loose with their subjects, flattering, enhancing and generally bending what they see to their artistic will. And why should we be any different?

How often it is that there are elements of a subject that detract from a picturesque ideal? An off-putting road sign or over hanging branch, a distracting background, a horrific pimple on a nose. If we were to reject any subject that was not perfect we would never get to draw anything. Whereas a photographer has to accept what he cannot physically alter, in drawing, we can simply pretend. I'll show you what I mean:

Here are two versions of the same scene. The first shows the scene as the camera would —everything in its right place, everything in its correct proportion. It's quite nice, but some parts are unsatisfying. Perhaps some of the issues could have been resolved by changing my viewpoint but, seeing as I was drawing from an upstairs window, that would have been tricky.

To draw the second version I put on my artist's hat. I moved the cottage round to a more picturesque angle, making up what I couldn't see. I greatly reduced the size of the trees surrounding and obscuring it and raised the height of the background hill to frame the cottage more elegantly. The fence came down in the frame slightly to give the cottage further breathing space and I changed it to a more rustic style, to suit the rural scene. I also shifted the telegraph pole further to the right, allowing it to extend clear above the distant hill.

Perhaps, in practice, you will not manipulate your subjects to quite this extent. The important thing is that you should feel free to make whatever alterations, omissions or enhancements that you feel moved to make. Drawings are not generally celebrated for their fidelity to reality so much as they are condemned for clumsy composition and distracting detail.

 Sprouts

This is a simple game for sophisticated minds. And punier brains too, you may be pleased to note. It was invented by mathematicians at Cambridge University, but even children can take to Sprouts (not the miniature cabbages, they hate them) as well as the boffins who have studied its complex mathematical properties.

Begin by drawing two dots in the middle of the page. The first player may draw a line between the dots or a circle from one dot back to the same dot. He/she then draws a new dot somewhere on the new line. Players then take turns to draw new curves, each time adding a new dot on the curve. There are three rules that govern play:

    1) No dot can have more than three lines attached to it.

    2) No line can cross another line.

    3) A new line cannot pass through a dot.

It will soon become impossible to add a new line and the first player to encounter this predicament is the loser and an abject failure of a human being. But this is one of those games in which the end can creep up unexpectedly and take even the victor by surprise, so perhaps they should not feel too smug.

TIP: For longer, more complex games, start with three, four, or more dots.

You will end up with some lovely designs and those that don't make it into frames for the parlour wall can be put to further use in playing the game Col (see 007). Then they'll look even prettier all shaded in.

(096) Exaggerate

From childhood we're told not to exaggerate. The word has acquired connotations of boastfulness and deceit, and on the lips of a fisherman or a politician those connotations may be well deserved. But where would our great storytelling tradition be without the odd conflation of reality? I would rather hear a good yarn than a precise account of provable facts. In art too we are seduced by subtle manipulations of subject matter. They make a drawing more interesting and more communicative. Exaggeration can be a good thing, and you should have no qualms about letting your pencil wander off into flights of fancy when the mood takes you.

The most obvious and easy way to exaggerate is with scale. Here's a stuffed fox from a museum. To my eye he looked rather pleased with his fine bushy tail, so in my drawing I made the tail larger to give it more emphasis.

What struck me about this cat was not so much its hairlessness and wrinkles as its oddly triangular head. I photographed it from very close up, to get the head almost filling the frame. In drawing it, I widened the top of the head and the space between the eyes and narrowed the mouth area to force it into a rigid geometry. In this way, exaggeration is very similar to caricature (see 020, 044, 072) and anthropomorphism (056).

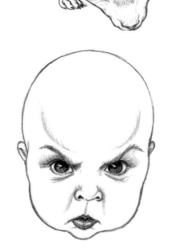

Here's my niece, again drawn from a photograph. She used to do a good line in contemptuous looks (actually, she still does), which I exaggerated here by emphasising the curves and shadows of her expressive eyebrows and her frowning mouth. Her hair was extremely fine, so I chose to leave it out altogether, for that dangerous, Bond villain look.

From the very young to the very old. When sketching our dear Nana I wanted to convey her extreme age (she's 98, you know), but not disrespectfully, I hope. I used firm, unforgiving marks throughout, reserving softer marks for her wispy hair alone. I emphasised the smallness and frailty of her body by exaggerating her slumped posture and making her head relatively large. I also widened the chair in which she sat to make her fill only a small part of it.

097 Draw a Circle

There is a legend about Michelangelo or Giotto or someone applying for a job to paint a ceiling or mural or something and demonstrating, as his credentials, a freehand drawing of a perfect circle. So impressed was the Pope or cardinal or whoever, at this feat of superhuman precision that he awarded the commission immediately. This story is probably a load of old hogwash, but it does tell us how the circle has been revered as a test of truly great draughtsmanship. Could you rise to the challenge of drawing a near perfect circle freehand? Would you put money on it? Here's how to make a few quid out of your mates.

After everyone has had a go and failed, hold your pencil in a writing grip, with a good couple of inches peeking out. Place your middle or ring finger firmly on the paper to act as a kind of axis and press the pencil's tip down. Now keep your drawing hand perfectly still. With your other hand, rotate the paper. When it has done a full turn, you will have a pretty well perfect circle on the page.

Mine's a pint of bitter, thanks.

098 Draw in the 4ᵗʰ Dimension

With your pencil you can capture the complete set of dimensions. A dot has no dimensions, a straight line only one, and a squiggle works in two dimensions. Most of the drawings in this book have dealt with the illusion of three dimensions, that is, the depiction of solid form and spatial depth. There is also a fourth dimension, influencing everything you draw. The fourth dimension is time.

You'll be familiar with the constraints of time, trying to finish a drawing before the light fades or before your subject moves. You may have discovered that restricting the length of time you allow for a drawing can produce surprisingly effective results. Perhaps you've tried to capture a sense of movement in a drawing, or sought to freeze the action and draw a single moment in time. But have you ever tried to draw a picture of time itself?

It's not quite so sci-fi as it may sound. Imagine, for example, drawing your garden in winter, neglected and bare. You could return to that drawing in spring and add some buds and blossom and gardening tools. In summer, some areas of full foliage and a paddling pool can be added and in the autumn the dead leaves scattered over the lawn. Thus a whole year of life can be contained in a single image.

But you needn't play such a long game. Here's a drawing I did whilst taking tea in a coffee shop. I first sketched the young couple, so intently gazing into each other's eyes that they paid me no attention. My daughter was similarly absorbed in her cake.

Then, as other customers came in and milled around the counter, I added them in roughly, one by one. Beyond that second layer of activity I then drew the staff behind the counter, placing them wherever there was a gap to fill.

As new people arrived, I could take from them details like coats and backpacks and develop the hastily sketched characters. By the time I had worked my way though a pot of tea (and very naughty cheesecake) the scene looked positively thronging and the young couple had long since moved on, presumably to find somewhere less public.

With the scene established, I could then take a few minutes to clean up and polish the drawing at my leisure. On the bus home I added a bit of shading, to give the scene a touch more atmosphere.

It would be impossible to draw a snap-shot of such a scene as it really took place, but you can set down a series of snapshots that fit together convincingly as a kind of heightened reality. It can be greatly rewarding to welcome chance happenings and allow them in one by one.

099 Keep a Sketchbook

When visiting a site of historical delight or natural splendour you may have noticed hordes all around you flashing away with their posh little cameras. Those snap-happy tourists are not really there, you know. Their bodies may be present, but their minds are focused on the unedited slideshows with full commentary they intend to inflict on the folks back home. But you are not like those Philistines, because you have a pencil and a sketchbook.

Sketching takes time. You can only realistically fill a few pages, at best, in a day—unless you are to antagonise your travelling companions. So you must be selective, which means that you look all the more intently at the wonders available to you, in search of suitable subjects. Perhaps, you'll go for quick, impressionistic panoramas, vignettes that encapsulate or typify your experience of the day, or you may be drawn to some quirky details that capture your imagination. Whatever subjects you select, you will be obliged to spend some quality time with them.

In the process of drawing, of studying and analysing what is before us, we do not merely look at things—we actually see them. And when we really see something, we get to know it, understand it and remember it.

Going through old sketchbooks rarely fails to prompt fond memories of long-forgotten locations, events and feelings. You will recall doing the drawings, the company you were in, the atmosphere and ambience of those experiences and the events surrounding them.

Sketchbooks take many forms: from unwieldy spiral-bound slabs down to tiny pocketsize notebooks. When choosing one, remember that you're going to have to cart it around with you. The A3 tome may look full of promise, but will it fit into your backpack? Can you comfortably support its open pages when jostling amongst the unyielding throng? I favour modest A5 (15cm x 21cm, 6" x 8") or A6 (10cm x 15cm, 4" x 6") hardback, book bound, sketchbooks – small enough to slip into a handbag or coat pocket. The hardback cover gives rigid support to both left and right pages when open, allowing one to draw across the entire spread. Most importantly, I beg you to resist the allure of cheaper models with a flimsy covers that bend as you struggle to draw on them.

Think of your sketchbook rather like your own private diary. Your sketches and notes need not mean anything to anyone else, nor do they need to be beautifully finished. It's a record of the things that catch your eye or inspire thought. Here are some pages from my visit to the Prado museum in Madrid: rough notes of painting details and compositions, and sketches of sculptures, some of which may one day provide inspiration for new drawings and illustrations.

After all that culture, my children were desperate to play in the park. Whilst they had their fun, I sketched a derelict kiosk. Having the sketchbook to hand helped me to pass the time and inspired me to look around for a satisfying subject that I would otherwise never have noticed.

TIP: A large rubber band stretched around the front cover and completed pages will stop them flapping in a breeze while you draw and also mark the page when the sketchbook is shut.

100 Compost

As a responsible citizen you will, of course, recycle your vegetable waste in a compost bin. And as an avid composter you will know that along with the 'green' waste that comes from the kitchen, lawn clippings and so on, good compost also requires an equal quantity of 'brown' matter, like dead leaves, cardboard and wood chips. So, rather than throwing your pencil shavings and stubs into the bin, save them for the compost heap. Now this may sound like one of the most futile pursuits known to man (and man knows some very futile pursuits), but just think: with two billion pencils being sold every year, that makes for an awful lot of landfill. So give your worms a treat and bask in the warm glow of righteousness.

101 The Ultimate Gesture

Being responsible citizens, we teach our youth that the path of violence is folly. But ever so rarely situations arise that can only be properly resolved by dishing out a good old punch in the gob. Likewise, although we have devoted many pages to building up our respect for the pencil, it may also be considered a powerful weapon for last-resort gestures of aggression.

In the cut and thrust of the meeting room you are only ever one barbed remark away from the veil of civility being torn down to reveal a hotbed of prejudice, ambition, apathy and conventional thinking. Against such a tide of negativity, the red-blooded champion of reason and fairness (you) must wield the pencil like a sword of justice. Waggle it in defiance, wave it dismissively, point it in direct challenge to your adversaries, and all the while maintain blood-chilling eye contact. Stab it, literally stab it into your notepad to emphasise your mightily impressive points. With such an armoury, how can the cause of righteousness be lost? Tragically, human stubbornness knows no bounds. If, in the end, your perfectly constructed arguments and passionate pleas fall on deaf ears you may need to crank things up to eleven.

You will have kept in reserve your ultimate gesture. Use it wisely, only in cases of extreme need, for once deployed there is no turning back. Make sure the stars are aligned: all eyes must be upon you, you must have the full attention of the assembly and you must have a clear passage to the exit. Build your closing speech to a rousing crescendo and as you reach your devastating final point, SNAP your pencil in two. There is nothing more to say.

You may now leave the room.

The End

. . .Or perhaps not. If in the midst of your performance you retain the presence of mind to keep hold of the broken parts, your pencil may live to fight another day. Carefully line up the ragged ends (they will of course be a precise fit for each other) and push them firmly back together. The wood grain will knit and hold quite well. Then wrap a short length of sticky tape very tightly around the join. There you are. Your most treasured tool will remain steadfast and rigid for many exciting exploits yet to come.

First published in 2014 by New Holland Publishers Pty Ltd
London • Sydney • Cape Town • Auckland

The Chandlery Unit 114 50 Westminster Bridge Road London SE1 7QY United Kingdom
1/66 Gibbes Street Chatswood NSW 2067 Australia
Wembley Square First Floor Solan Road Gardens Cape Town 8001 South Africa
218 Lake Road Northcote Auckland New Zealand

www.newhollandpublishers.com

A record of this book is held at the British Library and the National Library of Australia.

ISBN 9781742575247

Managing Director: Fiona Schultz
Publisher: Alan Whiticker
Project Editor: Emily Carryer
Designer: Keisha Galbraith
Production Director: Olga Dementiev
Printer: Toppan Leefung Printing Ltd (China)

10 9 8 7 6 5 4 3 2 1

Keep up with New Holland Publishers on Facebook
www.facebook.com/NewHollandPublishers

UK £12.99